WHAT PEOPLE
TH

M000113994

"A uniquely chilling tour
for any paranormal road-trip!"

Nicole Bray, Paranormal Michigan Book Series author

****

"Ghosts, spirits, and the unexplained...if you are brave
enough to seek out that which goes bump in the night, **The**
Michigan Road Guide to Haunted Locations *is a must-*
have guide to all things spooky and haunted in Michigan."

Kristy Robinett, Medium, Author and Owner of Michigan's
Haunted Hideaways

****

"Having researched the paranormal for nearly twenty
years, it is great to have a book like **The Michigan Road**
Guide to Haunted Locations *to share with those interest-*
ed in being part of the field. It provides clear, concise
details on the paranormal happenings in our state. It is a
road map to the supernatural."

Christopher Bailey, Research Director of Grimstone Inc.
Paranormal Investigators

****

*"***The Michigan Road Guide to Haunted Locations** *offers*
its readers a thrilling look at scores of haunted locations in
Michigan including eerie lighthouses, haunted inns and
restaurants and cemeteries where the dead may not rest.
Whether you are a dedicated paranormal investigator, a
weekend ghost hunter or a lover of true ghost stories, this
book is a must have."

Robin Lemkie, Founder, GHOSM - Ghost Hunters of Southern
Michigan

THE
MICHIGAN
ROAD GUIDE
TO

HAUNTED
LOCATIONS

THE
MICHIGAN
ROAD GUIDE
TO
HAUNTED
LOCATIONS

By Chad Lewis & Terry Fisk

Research Publishing Company
A Division of Unexplained Research, LLC

The Michigan Road Guide to Haunted Locations
by Chad Lewis and Terry Fisk

Unexplained Research Publishing Company
A Division of Unexplained Research LLC
P.O. Box 2173, Eau Claire, WI 54702-2173
Email: info@unexplainedresearch.com
www.unexplainedresearch.com

Copyright © 2013 by Chad Lewis and Terry Fisk
Printed in the United States by McNaughton, Gunn & Associates

Publisher's Cataloging-in-Publication

Lewis, Chad.
   The Michigan road guide to haunted locations / by Chad
Lewis & Terry Fisk ; foreword by Linda S. Godfrey.
   p. cm.
   LCCN 2013948595
   ISBN-13: 978-0-9798822-3-4
   1. Haunted places--Michigan--Guidebooks. 2. Ghosts--
Michigan--Guidebooks. 3. Legends--Michigan--Guidebooks.
4. Michigan--Guidebooks. I. Fisk, Terry. II. Title.
133.1'09774

Back Cover Photo: Rob Mattison

DEDICATION

This book is dedicated to Horatio Jackson- The first person to road trip the US from coast to coast.

—Chad

To Karen "Ku" Kuphal and Robert "Bob" Harvey, who introduced this night stalker to the night life of Michigan.

—Terry

TABLE OF CONTENTS

2 - Northwest **Michigan**   35

3 - Southeast **Michigan**   51

PREFACE

Corrections. Although we have made every effort to be certain this road guide is reliable and accurate, things inevitably change and errors are made. We appreciate it when readers contact us so we can revise future editions of the book.

Updates. If you have a paranormal experience at one of these locations, please report it to us. We recommend that you keep a journal, carefully recording dates, times, locations, and what happened.

Additions. Due to lack of space, many locations had to be left out of the book. We do intend to publish a second volume. Please write and let us know of any Michigan locations that you feel should have been included in this travel guide.

Warning. Be respectful of both the living and the dead. Several communities have had problems with people who go to these locations only to party and cause mischief. Cemeteries have been desecrated; private property has been vandalized; grounds have been littered; and buildings have been broken into.

If you do decide to check out any of the locations for yourself, please make sure that you have permission if it is private property and obey all applicable laws. Under most ordinances, cemeteries are only open from sunrise to sunset.

We will not be held responsible for any persons who decide to conduct their own investigations or for those who choose to break laws.

Disclaimer. The places listed in the book have neither been proved nor disproved to be haunted. Their inclusion in the book is based on the anecdotal reports we have received from numerous individuals. This book is for reference purposes only.

FOREWORD

BY

LINDA S. GODFREY

I don't claim to know what ghosts are, but I know Michigan has a lot of them. I put thousands of miles on my car driving the Upper and Lower Peninsulas in search of spooky places and legendary haunts for my books *Weird Michigan* and *Strange Michigan*, and I found these things in fetid abundance everywhere I went.

Michigan's incredible amount of Great Lakes shoreline gives it a huge head start over other states. With Great Lakes shores come lighthouses, and has there ever been a lighthouse that wasn't haunted? My two favorites, the Ontonagon and Seul Choix Lighthouses, not only are said to house lingering dead sea captains and light keepers, they provide mesmerizing tours of the restored properties, as well.

That summarizes much of what I like about Michigan. If the ghosts you are hoping to see don't show up, there's always an incredible view and a generous dollop of historic background to investigate. For instance, Michigan also contains the mother lode of cemeteries with scary backstories. There's a graveyard to suit every taste— from Detroit's huge, park-like Elmwood Cemetery with its legends of bloody eighteenth century battles and loup garous to the rural charm of the iron-fenced Reynolds Cemetery outside Jackson where lies the victim of an 1883 mass murder. I still get current reports of the glowing tombstone of Evart Cemetery in the middle of the Lower Peninsula.

FOREWORD

You'll also find any number of haunted hotels, inns, theaters, and other public places. I saw Basement Billy in Manistee, and found mysterious, melted candle wax on my camera after dining at the Felton Hotel—although there were no candles burning in the place. Michigan has the additional, happy tendency to leave large, abandoned institutions such as the former Northern Michigan Asylum in Traverse City mostly intact—along with some of their former residents, to judge by the tales told about them.

The very highways and byways you travel, especially those with bridges, are also likely to be known for phantom reminders of tragic pasts. The state has two Crybaby Bridges, one Hell's Bridge, and numerous other transits to the dark side—not to mention towns named Hell and Paradise. Of course, if you happen to chance upon one of Michigan's two "gravity roads," you may never get where you were going because your car will just keep getting sucked back uphill. Stop at Detroit's Knock Knock Road and you may be too afraid to continue, anyway. And while the stories of dead youths associated with Michigan's shoe trees are probably no more than urban legend, you toss your own Reeboks up into the mix at your own peril.

The hunt for Michigan's weird underbelly can be a wild ride, and it helps to have a well-researched guide to help you find Minnie Quay's Beach of Death or navigate the desolation of Blood Road. You especially need to know the most likely places you may need to slam on the brakes to avoid hitting a Michigan Dog Man. This Road Guide is an essential tool for all these things, and contains all the information your GPS will never know enough to tell you. If you leave home without it, well, never say I didn't warn you. But you may just give the devil another reason to scream at midnight on Hell's Bridge.

–Linda Godfrey is the author of *The Michigan Dogman: Werewolves and Other Canines Across the USA*, *Weird Michigan: Your Travel Guide to Michigan's Local Legends and Best Kept Secrets*, *Strange Michigan*, and many other books on strange and eccentric topics. Visit lindagodfrey.com for more.

ACKNOWLEDGMENTS

We would like to thank Jeannine Fisk, Linda Godfrey, Nisa Giaquinto, Sarah Szymanski, Lisa de Felice, Noah Voss, Kevin Nelson, and Sharon Price for assisting us with the research and production of this book.

We also want to thank the many people who provided us with cases, directions, and personal accounts.

CHAD'S INTRODUCTION

Adventure is worthwhile in itself.

—Amelia Earhart

Most people who travel through Michigan will have no trouble discovering "Uppers" and "pasties," but if you really want to break away from the throngs of sightseeing tourists you must take a detour from the heavily trodden paths to the lush underbelly of Michigan's darker side. Why suffer the monotony of the same old tourist draws when you have the option of discovering the lost spirits of Pere Cheney or the chance to come face to muzzle with the feared witchy wolves.

During my research travels through Michigan, I was taken aback by the wonderful variety of haunted places the state had to offer. On any given night, I could venture from a haunted lighthouse to a haunted graveyard to a haunted theater, all within a blood-curdling scream of one another. Whether I was in the UP or under the bridge, Michigan was littered with terrific haunted spots that celebrated a long history of supernatural happenings. Deep into the night I was able to investigate tales of a dead father and daughter meeting up for a ghostly family reunion, a historic hotel where departed guests refuse to depart, and a rural bridge that is home to a mysterious disembodied light. I also encountered my fair share of gruesome hauntings too, like the old summer camp where all the children were burnt to a crisp, or the secluded tomb where the town hermit stored his decaying relatives. But what surprised me the most during my travels of Michigan was the extent in which local people had kept these stories alive and well (unlike the people the cases were based on). Many of these stories dated back several decades, yet a large majority of people still vividly recalled the history, folklore, and family ties surrounding the bizarre tales.

I have to say that while planning my investigation route through Michigan I was a bit apprehensive. As a native of the state of Wisconsin, I was a bit afraid that Michigan would be too similar a place for me to really explore new terrain. How wrong I was! Granted, both states have a heavily forested north woods, both border the Great Lakes, and each are known for their friendly residents. But when I pushed through the obvious similarities I found that Michigan had a character all its own, complete with a huge treasure of folklore, superstitions, mysterious creatures, and supernatural occurrences that were as unique to the state as its people.

All of these factors add up to one hell of a great legend trip through Michigan. My advice is this. Gas up the car and cruise the countless back roads that allow you to prowl through the most hidden places of the state. Pack a bag and spend the night under the flickering glow of the neon sign at an old roadside motel. Grab some food at the local diner where townsfolk are just as likely to be discussing local legends as they are the weather. Visit some weird roadside attractions to provide your frazzled nerves a break from all the legend tripping. But above all else, have an adventure!

Keep an eye out,

Chad Lewis

TERRY'S INTRODUCTION

When you're safe at home
you wish you were having an adventure;
when you're having an adventure
you wish you were safe at home.

—Thornton Wilder

Shortly after they were married, my parents traveled from western Wisconsin to Michigan's Upper Peninsula for a little vacation. They had such a good time that—four children later—they decided to repeat the journey to share the experience with a whole new generation. I was twelve at the time, and was crammed into the backseat of the family car with my three younger siblings. In three hurried days, we traveled over 1,100 miles. Riding in the car for over 22 hours might have been unbearable, had it not been for the frequent stops to check out the tourist attractions and natural beauty of the Wolverine State. Our parents brought us to scenic places such as Lake of the Clouds in the Porcupine Mountains, and we also saw several waterfalls, including Tahquamenon Falls in Paradise, which is one of the largest waterfalls in Michigan and second largest east of the Mississippi. Other stops included the Soo Locks in Sault Ste. Marie, Marquette (the largest city in the U.P.), and Fayette Historic State Park.

On our trip we also encountered things that I found "magical." There was a tiny village named Christmas, where they celebrated the holiday season all year round. The streets there bore names such as St. Nicholas Street, Mistletoe Lane, Jingle Bell Way, and

Scrooge's Alley. Although we were there in July, most residents still displayed their Christmas lights and decorations. Other places, like Kitchitikipi in Manistique, with its tales and Indian legends, had a mystical or spiritual feel to it. This small lake is Michigan's largest natural freshwater spring, and has a self-operated observation raft that allows you view the bottom, 40 feet down, through the crystal-clear waters. Taking the ferry to Mackinac Island, where cars are banned, was almost like traveling backwards through time to an era before the automobile. Touring the island's fort took us even further back in time. The "world famous" Mystery Spot of St. Ignace is a rustic cabin on a "gravity hill." Although the tourist attraction is a tilt-induced visual illusion, it still remains impressive and fun.

With the fond childhood memories of my family vacation, I could not wait to return as an adult to relive some of those memories. I still found Michigan to be magical and otherworldly. People ate strange foods there, like pasties, and even spoke differently, referring to tourists as "fudgies" and liquor stores as "party stores" and ballpoint pens as "ink pens." As a farewell, they commonly uttered the expression "Have a good one!"

Michigan's state motto is *Si quaeris peninsulam amoenam circumspice* (If you seek a pleasant peninsula, look about you). It could just as easily be "If you seek a haunted location, look about you," since that's what I quickly discovered as I trekked across the state. Even if an investigation turned out to be a deadend, I had local people giving me dozens of other leads to haunted locations.

It was also my observation that in Michigan some types of hauntings are more common than in other states. I've noticed this pattern with other states as well, as each state seems to have a common theme when it comes to hauntings. With South Dakota it's Native Americans, with Illinois it's gangsters, with Iowa it's cursed cemetery statues, and with Michigan it's haunted lighthouses. This probably shouldn't come as a surprise to anyone, since the state does have 3,126 miles of Great Lakes shoreline (more fresh water coastline than any other state). The State Nickname is the "Great Lake State," and anywhere in Michigan, you are within 85 miles of one of the Great Lakes. In fact, it's the only state that touches four of the five Great Lakes. With about 115 lighthouses, Michigan has more than any other state, and each of them has a unique look and story—usually a ghost story. Some of these lighthouses still shine for ships, others are abandoned or serve as museums or bed and breakfasts.

In addition to the lighthouses, we've investigated other types of haunted places. We've searched for public places that the reader can visit firsthand, and we've tried to find places with a long history of haunting activity with multiple eyewitnesses accounts. If the reader is interested in having their own haunting experience, this book will tell them where to go. On the other hand if that type of thing terrifies the reader, the book will tell them where *not* to go.

Have a good one!

Terry Fisk

NORTHEAST MICHIGAN

Camp 8 Cabin

Location: Atlanta, Montmorency County, Michigan
Address: Camp 8 Road, Atlanta, MI 49709

Directions: From Atlanta take Hwy. 32 (M32) to the west toward Bigelow. Turn right on Camp 8 Road. Follow this road until you come to Old State Road intersection. The old vacant cabin will be on the corner of Camp 8 Rd. and Old State Rd. on your right side, just past the stop sign. This is a private home; please view from road.

Ghost Lore

It seems like every run-down abandoned building eventually becomes known as the town's haunted house. Filled with a scary back story, a tragic history, and a fair share of bizarre tales, the legend only multiplies as time passes by. One such place is the old deserted cabin on Camp 8 Road. Here the haunted legend has been brewing for quite some time. It was inside the house that three young sisters went crazy and took their own lives at the end of a rope in the upstairs bedroom. Or wait…did the girls perish in the upstairs room when the flu epidemic passed through town? No one really seems to know, but that hasn't stopped the legend of this old cabin from continuing to grow.

- The ghostly images of several young children can be seen peeking at you from the upstairs windows.

- The place is plagued by mysterious screams and crying that are heard coming from inside the empty house.

History

1918 – An influenza epidemic swept through the town and took many lives. Two young girls died in their family's small two-story cabin.

Little is known about the history of the cabin. It is believed that the wooden cabin was used by loggers in the area.

Investigation

We spoke with a woman whose husband works as the caretaker of the corner cabin. The woman told us that, according to the current property owner, there once was a small two-story cabin on the land. It was in this cabin that the two young girls did indeed die when the flu epidemic passed through. It was said that after the death, the family moved out of the house to the town of Gaylord. The house where the girls died is no longer there.

This odd story has been circulating the area for many years. In the 1970s, a group of young friends ventured out to the cabin in search of the legend. It was a dark and misty night and a dense fog hung over the land. Through the fog the group noticed two small red eyes peering back at them. The group watched in amazement and swore that the mysterious eyes blinked twice and then simply disappeared back into the fog.

Although the original home where the young girls perished is no longer standing, many believe that their spirits still reside in the area. Late at night, visitors often hear the creepy sound of young girls crying coming from inside the vacant cabin. On some evenings, witnesses say that the soft cries sound more like chilling screams.

We also received a lot of reports of cameras capturing weird phenomena while out at the cabin. Many people like to take a lot of photos of the cabin and the surrounding area, hoping to see if they can capture an image of the ghostly activity. When the photos are later analyzed, strange orbs and mysterious balls of light can be seen in them.

The Lost Village of Pere Cheney

Location: Beaver Creek Township, Crawford County, Michigan

Directions: Head north on Hwy 18 and then turn left on Chase Bridge Road. Follow this for approximately 4 miles, then turn left on Pere Cheney Road (dirt road). Follow this all the way until you reach the T, then turn left on Stanley Lake Road. Turn right on Railroad St. and in ½ mile you will be able to see the cemetery right across from the railroad tracks. You can stop there and walk over the tracks on your left to the cemetery. You can also keep driving to the stop sign, turn left and pass over the tracks. Then take your immediate left and you can drive into the cemetery.

Ghost Lore

In the early days of Michigan, the village of Pere Cheney was a bustling little place chalked full of people and commerce.

Unfortunately, tragedy struck in the 1800s when the village was ravaged by diphtheria. In order to stop the spread of this horrible disease, it was decided that what was remaining of the town would be burned. The people quickly rebuilt their homes and businesses and the village once again thrived. However, the prosperity was short lived as a second deadly wave of disease again tore through the village and ripped apart families. Talk soon spread that the town was cursed and that people should get out while they still could. By the early 1900s the town was completely abandoned, and the only remaining evidence of the existence of the ghost town is the Pere Cheney Cemetery, and of course the ghosts.

- The cemetery is haunted by a witch that was hanged and burned in the cemetery.

- The inhabitants of the cursed place are forever doomed to roam the last remaining part of their town.

- The surrounding woods are alive with strange sounds and mysterious noises.

- Visitors who are foolish enough to steal from the cemetery are cursed with bad luck.

History

1870 – The Village of Pere Cheney was settled. The settlement was named after G. M. "Papa" Cheney, who constructed the first sawmill in the area. The town was mostly made up of lumberjacks and sawmill workers.

1879 – Pere Cheney became the county seat for a short period of time.

1881 – The census of Pere Cheney listed the population at 922. The Michigan Central Railroad established a track line that ran through Pere Cheney. The town enjoyed a hotel, Western Union, school, depot, several sawmills, and the C.S. Hutt general store.

1883 – Disease spread through the town. Diphtheria ravaged the town, killing many children.

1893 – The town was hit with smallpox, scarlet fever, and diphtheria.

1906 – Diphtheria once again ravaged the town.

1911 – The Pere Cheney post office closed down.

1914 – The town was nearly deserted.

1918 – Only 18 residents remained in Pere Cheney. The cemetery had been vandalized, with numerous graves destroyed.

1989 – The Grayling branch of the VFW started the process of cleaning the cemetery. Graves were put back together, the field was cut, and a flag pole was put up.

Source: *Ghost Towns of Michigan Vol. 2* by Larry Wakefield

Investigation

Nearly everyone we spoke with was familiar with the story of the cursed town of Pere Cheney. The town did suffer several major outbreaks of disease that killed off a large number of the residents, as evidenced by a cemetery full of those who perished in the outbreaks.

During our investigation we found no evidence that the town was purposely burned down or that the residents thought it was cursed. A more convincing explanation of the town's demise is that the people simply started moving to the bigger cities of Grayling and Roscommon to find better employment opportunities and Pere Cheney slowly vanished.

Most young people in the area have ventured out to the country to try and locate the Pere Cheney Cemetery, which is the only remaining piece of the town. It is a place where many teens go to party away from the watchful eyes of their parents or the police. One group of friends told us that several years ago they went out to the cemetery to camp and party. It was a long night and numerous beers had been consumed and discarded throughout the cemetery when the group finally drifted off to sleep. When the blazing sun finally awoke the sleeping teens they noticed that all the beer cans had been picked up and thrown neatly into the garbage can. They believed that the spirits had cleaned up the cemetery while they slept.

A local man in his 40s said that he would often go to the cemetery to look at the old graves. Every time that he walked through the cemetery he would get the feeling that he was not alone, and on many occasions he saw strange figures moving around the cemetery.

One of the most popular legends of the place involves a woman who lived in Pere Cheney. Townsfolk believed that the woman was a witch, so they dragged her from town and brought her to the cemetery where she was hanged and burned on a tree. Although we found no actual accounts of a "witch" being hanged and burned in the cemetery, we did speak with several witnesses who told similar stories of seeing the ghostly image of a woman hanging from a tree inside the cemetery.

The Dare. If you take any object from the cemetery, you will be cursed with bad luck until the item is returned.

Heikie's Tomb

Location: Cheboygan, Cheboygan County, Michigan
Address: Orchard Road, Cheboygan, MI 49721

Directions: Heikie's Tomb is notoriously hard to find. It is also on private property, so please view from road or get permission to visit.

From Cheboygan head west on Hwy. 23 (E. State St.). Turn right on Butler Rd. and follow it to Orchard Rd. Turn left on Orchard and follow it until you are forced to make a left turn, but do not turn left. Instead, you will see a dirt road straight ahead of you. Go straight, follow the road, and take your first right. You will pass by Misty Morning Lane on your right. At approximately 1.7 miles the road will fork. You want to go to the left and you will come to a wired gate where the private property begins.

The Tomb: If you have permission, get out of your vehicle and walk to the newly constructed wood pavilion and cabin.

Turn right here and walk towards the woods. The small path will fork, so turn to the left and the tomb will be on your immediate left in the bushes.

The Well: If you have permission, get out of your vehicle and walk to the newly constructed wood pavilion and cabin. Turn left and walk about 20 feet into the woods and you will see the remains of the well.

Ghost Lore

Out in the middle of the woods there was an old secluded cabin where a strange recluse lived all alone. Townsfolk feared this hermit, and rumors soon spread that he lived out there by himself because he had brutally murdered his wife and children. After killing off his family the man began receiving religious visions that persuaded him to gather rocks from the surrounding countryside and build grottos and various other monuments to Jesus. The deranged man also used the rocks to build a burial tomb for himself.

- Those who are brave enough to remove pieces of the dead man's tomb will be cursed with bad luck and die within a short period of time.

- The whole area is surrounded by thick brush and clustered trees and late at night unknown noises can be heard moving through the dark woods.

- The tomb is a hotbed of paranormal activity. On many nights a fog-like apparition of a man stands in front of the tomb watching over his creation.

History

1950s – The well, tomb, and several other alters were created by Mr. Heikie. Local legends stated that he created the grottos because he was a very religious man.

1960s – It is believed that Mr. Heikie passed away during this time. The cause of his death is not known.

Today – The Heikie family is using the land as a hunting cabin.

Investigation

There are several different versions of this old legend. First, the place is almost always wrongly referred to as Hikyes Tomb, when in fact the correct name is Heikie's Tomb. We have also found that some families use an alternate spelling of 'Heike.'

The man who owned the land was Stan Heikie. His grandson gave us a tour of the land that he now owns. He told us that the story passed on to him was that his grandfather loved his land so much that he constructed the tomb with the hopes of one day being buried inside of it. The grandson had no information as to the cause of his grandfather's death. Since the grandson is still living and the linage continues, it is very unlikely that Heikie killed his wife and children.

When the rock tomb was originally constructed, it stood over ten feet tall and contained the handprints and footprints of Heikie. Over the years, the tomb has shrunk considerably due to frequent thefts and vandalism.

As far as we were able to learn, Stan passed away sometime in the early 1960s. The grandson believes that the tomb, the well, and the now demolished alters were built sometime in the 1950s.

It appears that this legend has been passed down through the community for many years. Nearly everyone we spoke with in town was familiar with the legend, but no one could recall how to get to the tomb.

We spoke with a local man who, 40 years ago, as a teenager, drove to the tomb with a buddy who lived out in that area. As they approached the tomb, his buddy told him that Heikie was just an old peaceful man who liked to keep to himself, and not the evil murderer the legends made him out to be.

Several other residents recalled going out to the tomb as teenagers only to be frightened away by the appearance of a transparent looking man standing over the tomb.

Many visitors to the area have unwisely decided to steal a piece of the tomb. Once the rock has been removed from the tomb the visitor's luck seems to take a turn for the worse. Over the years, reports of vehicles mysteriously stalling, unexplained bad luck, and tragic accidents have all been blamed on the stolen rocks.

The Dare. If you grab a rock or piece of stone from the tomb or well, you will be cursed with bad luck until the stone is properly returned.

Capitol Theater

Location: Flint, Genesee County, Michigan
Address: 140 East Second Street, Flint,MI 48502-1731
Phone: (810) 767-5141

Directions: From Interstate 475 take Highway 21 (East Court St.) to the west. Turn right on S. Saginaw St., follow it to East Second St., take a right, and you will see the theater.

Ghost Lore

The next time you head off to enjoy a new movie, take a good look at the theater you are in. Marvel at the spacious ceilings, the ornate carving on the walls, and the lush velvet seats. Wait a minute, you've probably noticed that the new 25-screen multiplex where we watch movies doesn't include any of these amenities. But, if you are looking for a nicer viewing experience, you need to visit a theater with some history, and one such place is the Capitol Theater

13

in downtown Flint. Years ago this historic 2000-seat theater was the heart of downtown Flint, and at one time it was filled with laughter, excitement, and life. Unfortunately, for the past few years the beautiful theater has only been filled with dust and ghosts.

- A worker was accidentally sealed in the wall and he frequently taps on the walls seeking your help.

- The spirit of a former usher continues to guide people to their seats.

History

1920s – W. S. Butterfield saw that the Flint community was in need of a grand theater. Mr. Butterfield hired architect John Eberson to construct the theater in a Mediterranean style.

1928 – On January 19th, the new Capitol Theater celebrated its grand opening in downtown Flint.

1933 – The Hal Roach Beauty and Personality Contest was held at the Capitol Theater. The winner of the competition was Marie Ann Callahan.

1977 – George Farah purchased the theater.

1985 – The theater was placed on the National Register of Historical Places.

2004 – A new $100,000 theater renovation project began with the help of a $50,000 matching grant from Detroit's downtown facade program.

2007 – The theater's marquee was fully renovated and was restored to its proper working condition.

2007 – The theater's marquee was featured in the Hollywood movie *Semi-Pro*.

2009 – The manager, Troy Farah, continued to oversee renovation of the theater.

Today – The theater is closed to the public and under renovation. The manager estimated that an additional $20-$30 million is needed to complete the restoration.

Investigation

On our visit to the theater we spoke with the manager who told us that, although he has never personally witnessed anything out of the ordinary in the theater, every year he receives hundreds of inquiries about the theater's haunted reputation.

Linda Godfrey, in her book *Weird Michigan,* included a letter from a reader who had heard stories that the theater was haunted by the wandering spirit of a former worker that had often been seen walking around the inside of the building.

A more sinister version of the deceased worker legend tells of a former employee who died when he was accidentally sealed inside one of the walls. It is said today that if you listen real close you can still hear the man's spirit knocking and tapping, trying to summon

your help from inside the walls. We were unable to locate any public story of a theater employee being sealed in the walls.

Back in the 1980s and 90s, the theater was a hotbed of live music. College students would often flock to the theater to party, drink, and enjoy some live music. It was during this time that a lot of the paranormal activity occurred. Visitors would often see the spirit of an usher walking through the theater as though he was leading someone to their seat. Witnesses said that the man was dressed in an usher's uniform and looked like he was from the early 1900s.

After many of the music shows ended, the staff would often stick around to clean up the place so they could eventually close up and go home. During these late nights, the staff would often hear the faint sounds of people laughing and talking up in the balcony. Thinking that maybe some people were still hanging out in the theater, the staff would walk up to the balcony only to find it completely empty and deathly quiet.

Dice Road Cemetery and Bridge

Location: Hemlock, Saginaw County, Michigan
Address: Dice Road, Hemlock, MI (near Saginaw)

Directions: Cemetery- Dice Rd. is only a couple mile stretch of road. Start on the east end and follow it to the west until you come to a house at 15727 Dice Road (between N. Hemlock Rd. and Fern Rd.). The cemetery will be across the street.

Bridge- The bridge is approximately ½ mile east of the cemetery. If you come from the east you will pass the bridge before you get to the cemetery.

Ghost Lore

Dice Road is one of those weird places that a lot of people have heard about, but few have actually visited. Dice Road is somewhat unique in the fact that not only does it have a haunted cemetery, but it has a haunted bridge as well. The stories of the road vary from visitors experiencing nothing out of the ordinary, to people getting so scared that they vow never to return. Hopefully your experience ends up somewhere in the middle.

- Two young girls were murdered in the cemetery and their lifeless bodies were hanged from the bridge.

- Devil worshippers use the cemetery to perform satanic rituals that include animal sacrifices.

- Something lurks in the trees and bushes that surround the cemetery. At night something can be seen and heard moving quickly through the brush.

- The spirit of a young woman in a flowing white dress haunts the bridge.

- The area wreaks havoc on vehicles. Reports of cars stalling, not starting, and headlights going out occur on a nightly basis.

History

1890 –   The St. Peter's Church congregation purchased 20 acres of land from Carl and Emile Rohde to be used as the Richland Lutheran Cemetery.

2003 –   The bridge was replaced over Whitmore Drain.

2006 –   The new section of the cemetery was developed. It was laid out by Larry Wolfgran, David Earley, and Joe McQueen.

Investigation

This case involves both the bridge and the cemetery. Most people refer to the cemetery as Dice Cemetery; however, the correct name is the Richland Lutheran Cemetery.

The cemetery and bridge have a long history of being haunted. We spoke with a woman who had lived in the area for over 40 years. She remembered hearing stories of young kids going out to the road during the 1960s. She stated that Dice Road was/is a popular party place for teenagers.

One of the best-known legends of the area is the story of two girls who spent the evening hanging out in the cemetery. Sometime during the night, an unknown man appeared, and when the morning sun broke the lifeless bodies of the two girls were discovered hanging from the bridge. Many people that visit the diminutive bridge wonder how two bodies could have been hanged from it. However, keep in mind that the bridge you see today not the original bridge. In 2003, the old bridge was replaced by the current bridge. Residents from the area say that the previous bridge was an old steel trussed bridge with overhanging steel trusses that would have had plenty of room to string up a body on.

The bridge is also the site where many visitors encounter the ghostly spirit of a mysterious woman. The apparition of the woman usually appears at night and it reported to be clothed in a long

flowing white dress. Those lucky enough to catch a glimpse of the woman say that she does not remain visible for long for as soon as she is spotted she disappears into the night. The identity of the vanishing woman is not known.

The cemetery is also a hotbed of paranormal activity. One of the most common experiences at the cemetery takes place in the surrounding woods. Those who walk around the cemetery have seen the hazy outline of some unknown person or creature lurking among the trees. This unknown entity can be heard breaking twigs and tree branches as it maneuvers about the woods.

Adding to the haunted reputation of the cemetery is the sense of dread and evil that overcomes many visitors. Those who have been there believe that something inside the cemetery is evil and warn that those who dare go there are putting themselves in danger.

The most common report we receive about the cemetery involves people immediately getting the feeling that they are not welcome there. Most people try to simply shrug off the uneasy feeling, chalking it up to their overactive nerves. However, those who decide to stay report being watched by some unseen presence. As the night progresses the feeling of dread intensifies until the visitor reaches a breaking point and can no longer remain in the cemetery.

One of the more puzzling aspects of the cemetery is the bizarre manner in which vehicles are affected. Normally, highly reliable cars seem to malfunction while traveling on Dice Road. We have received cases of cars having trouble starting, electrical problems, headlights mysteriously ceasing to work, trouble starting, and even cars dying while in the area.

J & B's Spot Bar & Grill

Location: Johannesburg, Otsego County, Michigan
Address: 1060 M 32, Johannesburg, MI 49751-9590
Phone: (989) 786-2471

Directions: The bar is located off of M 32 in the small town of Johannesburg. It is right next to Vienna Corners and approximately 19 miles west of Atlanta.

Ghost Lore

As you travel the back roads of America, you really get a chance to discover some unique small businesses that are all hidden from interstate travelers. Far from the cookie-cutter looks and designs of the big national chains, these wonderful places are often overflowing with both character and history. J & B's Bar & Grill is one such place. A combination of an old car service station and one-room schoolhouse, this is one place where you can enjoy some ghostly spirits along with your food and spirits.

21

- A former owner of the bar continues to monitor the bar's visitors and employees, even from his grave.

- Unknown voices can be heard calling out for both staff and visitors.

History

1890s – The original building was constructed to be used as a car service and repair shop.

1946 – The service repair shop had closed. Joe and Nettie Buc purchased the business and operated it as "The Spot Bar." The name was chosen due to the fact that during Prohibition an illegal still was located behind the building. The townsfolk secretly referred to the place where they purchased their liquor as "The Spot."

1950 – The bar was purchased by Stanley Krol. Mr. Krol purchased an old one-room schoolhouse as an addition to the building. During the winter, the schoolhouse was hauled to The Spot by a horse drawn sleigh.

1964 – After the death of Stanley Krol, the business was purchased by Michael Johnston. During this time, many of the bar's customers were in the area for recreation and hunting.

1983 – Jim and Sawn Sokoloski bought the business. The couple decided the bar needed to expand its food choices so a new full kitchen was constructed. The couple also completely annexed the remaining portion of the building and used it as a large seating area.

1997 – The bar was sold to Judy and Bill Pappas. The name was changed to J&B's Bar and Grill.

Today– The bar and grill is open to the public and is known for its tasty food.

Investigation

The main belief and legend is that the establishment is haunted by the ghost of former owner Stanley Krol who died while working in the building.

Former owners of the bar have reported many strange occurrences that took place inside the building. On many occasions, items would simply disappear, only to reappear sometime later in a completely different location. It was also common for the owners to clearly hear a person calling out their name, only to discover that they were alone in the building. Several different times the witness was so shaken by the eerie experience that they bolted out the door, while calling it quits for the day.

The current owners told us that not only were they familiar with the legends of the place being haunted, they even had their own firsthand experiences. It appears that they too have heard mysterious voices inside the bar. One day two women were working in the building when the boss heard the other woman call out, "Have you opened the front door yet?" Thinking it was a

weird thing to say the boss asked the woman what she had meant. The stunned woman stated that she had not said anything. Later that same day, the roles would reverse when the other woman heard the boss calling out for her. When she found the boss she asked what she had wanted and was told that the boss had not uttered a word. The two women were completely puzzled by the fact that they were the only two people inside the building, where the other voices came from still remains a mystery.

Both staff and visitors have reported seeing the apparitions of several ghostly figures standing in the older portion of the building. The apparitions are never seen clearly enough to discover who they might be.

The Witchy Wolves of Omer Plains

Location: Omer, Arenac County, Michigan

Directions: Head west out of Omer and turn right on North Michigan Street. North Michigan will turn into Jose. Follow Jose back into the woods and this whole area is considered the Omer Plains.

Ghost Lore

Omer's claim to fame is that it is officially the smallest city in Michigan. The irony is that the state's smallest city is home to one of Michigan's biggest legends. Today the sparse rural town is surrounded by heavily wooded forests. Yet years ago the land was inhabited by a Native American tribe. As the white pioneers began settling the area, the tribe called upon the protective spirits of the Witchy Wolf to protect them from the encroachment of the white man. The Witchy Wolf spirits laid dormant for many years until an

25

old Native American burial ground was disturbed. Since then, these half-man/half-wolf spirits have been seen terrorizing the plains and protecting the resting Native American spirits.

- A ferocious spirit animal attacks those brave enough to get out and explore the Omer Plains.

- Over the years several people have mysteriously vanished in the plains while looking for the creature.

History

1800s – The band of Chippewa lived in the area. They used the Omer Plains area for several of their burial grounds.

1860s – The town of Omer was founded by George Gorie and George Carscallen. The town was originally named Rifle River Mills. The town was going to be renamed Homer, but such a place already existed in Michigan so the "H" was simply dropped to Omer.

1903 – The town of Omer was incorporated as a city.

1950s – The area was known as the Witchy Willow and was a popular place for teenagers to go "parking."

1960s – Stories began surfacing of the Witchy Wolf ripping the stockings of women who visited the area.

1980s – The area served as a hotspot for young people to gather and party.

Investigation

The area of Omer Plains is said to house the protective spirit of a half-man/half-wolf that patrols the area. The Witchy Wolf spirit is thought to be a hairy biped, as it is most often seen running upright on its hind legs. It is believed that many years ago the Chippewa who lived in the area summoned the spirit of this creature to protect the area from any harm.

Although many people refer to the Witchy Wolf as a werewolf type creature, old legends and eyewitness sightings seem to contradict this assumption. Most legends refer to the creature as being some type of spirit and not simply an unknown flesh and blood creature. Many eyewitnesses claim that the creature they saw was some mixture of both man and wolf which would exclude the possibility of a mistaken Bigfoot creature.

Adding even more mystery to this baffling case is the fact that while the creature is often heard, it is rarely seen. Most of the witnesses report hearing the growls and howling of some type of creature, yet no animal can be seen with the naked eye. What truly scares visitors is the fact that people who hear these eerie growls have reported being knocked down by some unseen force.

During the 1940s and 50s, teenagers often used the secluded area as a place to go "parking." Women started coming back with their stockings ripped and claimed to have been attacked by the Witchy Wolf. On one occasion, a young woman and her boyfriend were parked out in the area when the girl walked into the woods to go to the bathroom. The young man was surprised when his girlfriend

came running back in a fit of terror and told him that some unknown creature had attacked her. The boyfriend ran into the woods to investigate and was immediately stopped in his tracks by the loud eerie howl of some unknown animal. The couple was so spooked that they torn off out of the area without further investigation.

We spoke with a local historian in his 60s who had lived in the area his entire life. He agreed to give us a tour of the Omer plains. While out on the tour we were told that the man remembered hearing the legend of the odd creatures when he was just a small child. The man brought us to several long-forgotten native burial grounds. It is thought that the disturbance of these graves in the early 1900s caused the spirits of the Witchy Wolves to appear.

Several reports claim that after spending time out in the woods looking for the creatures, people have returned to their vehicles only to discover strange scratch and claw marks on their doors and roofs.

We spoke with several young Omer residents who warned us of the many dangers of going out looking for the Witchy Wolves. They told us that we needed to be extremely careful because they had heard stories of thrill-seeking kids who drove out to the plains in search of the Witchy Wolves. These young people were never heard from again.

The town seems to embrace the old legend, as each January the "Witchy Wolf Run" is held on a full moon evening. Over fifteen miles of rugged terrain and many scary surprises await the adventurous runners of this popular night adventure race.

The Dare. If you go out looking for the Witchy Wolves, you will never return.

Presque Isle Lighthouse

Location: Presque Isle, Presque Isle County, Michigan
Address: 5295 East Grand Lake Road,
Presque Isle, MI 49777
Phone: (989) 595-2787

Directions: From Rogers City take US 23 South and turn left
(east) on Hwy. 638. Stay to the left at the fork still traveling on
638. Turn north on Grand Lake Road and follow it and the
entrance for the park will be on your right. Park your car and
walk the path to the lighthouse and museum.

Ghost Lore

Lighthouses play an essential role in the safekeeping of passing
ships. Night and day, these lights provide safe passage to ships and
sailors looking to come into the harbor. Years ago, light keepers
were trusted to perform the necessary upkeep and maintenance to

ensure that the lights functioned properly and thus the ships arrived safely. Keepers took their jobs seriously, knowing that other people's lives depended on them. The light keeper at Presque Isle Lighthouse took his job so seriously that he continued to perform it from his grave.

- On dark, stormy nights the ghost of a former light keeper will guide sailors safely into shore.

- A mysterious spirit will bunker down in the cabin and spend the night in one of the beds.

- The phantom scent of breakfast drifts through the inside of the cabin.

History

1838 – State Representative Isaac Crary petitioned for funding for the construction of a lighthouse. Congress granted his wish and allocated $5,000 for the construction of the Presque Lighthouse.

1839 – A construction agreement was signed by Abraham Wendell, the U.S. Superintendent of Lighthouses, and contractor Jeremiah Moore. The agreed upon price of the lighthouse was $5,000.

1840 – The lighthouse was completed and certified by Mr. John Scott.

1840 – Henry Woolsey was appointed the first keeper of the lighthouse. Mr. Woolsey's annual pay was set at $350.

1868 – The lighthouse keeper's house was in need of major renovations. Plans were drawn up to renovate the home. However, it was determined that the location of the lighthouse did not best suit the needs of the harbor, so congress appropriated $28,000 for the construction of a new lighthouse to be built at the north end of the peninsula.

1897 – The lighthouse was decommissioned. The lighthouse was put up for auction with the highest bid coming from Edward O. Avery.

1899 to 1901 – The lighthouse was sold to General Duffield, who then sold it to Bliss Stebbins for $70,000.

1930 – The property was sold to Francis Stebbins. Francis planned to use the property as a summer cottage for his family.

1930s – Francis discovered that the house was so dilapidated that it would be much easier to simply tear it down and start fresh with a new one. Francis began construction of the new home and used salvaged beams from the old Lansing Post Office for the floor and ceiling.

1965 – The lighthouse was dedicated with a State Historical Marker.

1969 – Francis Stebbins passed away and his son James Stebbins inherited the property.

1977 – George and Loraine Parris were hired as live-in tour guides and caretakers.

1992 – George Parris passed away after suffering a heart attack. His wife Lorraine remained at the lighthouse as caretaker.

1995 – Jim Stebbins sold the property to the State of Michigan for the site of a museum and park.

2003 – Lorraine stopped working at the museum and retired.

Today – The museum is open to the public for tours.

Source: Presque Isle Lighthouse

Investigation

It is believed that the ghost of George Parris is continuing to operate the lighthouse, even though he died in 1992. Soon after George's death, witnesses began to notice a light emanating from the lighthouse. It should be noted that after the new lighthouse was built, the old tower light was deactivated and parts were removed to ensure that it would not accidentally turn on.

The first report of the phantom light came from George's wife Lorraine, who spotted a bright light coming from the tower as she was driving to work, but as she got close to the cabin the light simply vanished. After having the bizarre incident repeat itself several times, Lorraine finally contacted the Coast Guard to see if they could clear up the mystery. The Coast Guard did show up and explained to Lorraine that it would be impossible for the light to shine due to the previous removal of numerous mechanical parts that were essential in the operation of the light.

Over the years various fishermen and women have contacted the museum to report their sightings of the light. Most state that while they were out fishing on the lake they caught a glimpse of what appeared to be a light shining brightly from the tower of the lighthouse.

A museum volunteer told us that one day a 12-year-old girl hurried in to the cabin to ask her mother if it was okay for her to go and explore the lighthouse. A short time later, the young girl returned to the cabin and was laughing. Her mother asked her what was so

funny, and the little girl said she had been speaking with the old light keeper in the tower and that he was really funny. The puzzled mother did not believe her daughter's story until the young girl excitedly pointed to a picture of George hanging on the wall and said, "That's him."

Bizarre activity is not strictly limited to the lighthouse, as many unexplained events have transpired inside the old cabin as well. When George and Lorraine resided in the cabin, George would always wake up early and make a nice breakfast for the couple. After George's death, Lorraine would often show up for work only to find that the museum smelled like George was still making breakfast. Lorraine noted that the scent of the phantom breakfast would only last a few minutes.

It also appears that George's spirit still enjoys spending the night at the cabin, because on many occasions a volunteer has shown up for work in the morning, only to discover that one of the cabin's beds was ruffled up as though someone had slept on top of the covers.

NORTHWEST MICHIGAN

The Blue Pelican Inn

Location: Central Lake, Antrim County, Michigan
Address: 2535 N. Main St., Central Lake, MI 49622-9270
Phone: (231) 544-BLUE (2583)
Fax: (231) 544-6737
Email: blue@thebluepelican.com
Website: www.thebluepelican.com
Facebook: www.facebook.com/TheBluePelicanInn

Ghost Lore

With a population of just under a thousand people, the village of
Central Lake is billed as "The Best Small Town in Northern
Michigan." If you're looking for the best place for lodging, the
locals will tell you it's definitely the Blue Pelican Inn. It has "Seven
Rooms of Distinction," the Pelican's Nest Restaurant, the Side
Door Saloon, and perhaps a friendly ghost or two.

- A man and woman dressed in late '20s, early '30s clothing has been seen.

- The ghost of an elderly man referred to as "Roy" has been seen in a bathroom on the second floor.

- Spooky organ music has been heard playing at night.

- Doorknobs will rattle.

- Snuffed out candles will ignite on their own.

- The dumbwaiter will deliver upside down plates to the bar.

- The night crew has heard muffled sounds, banging, and light scratching. When they call out to the noises, they stop.

- An apparition was seen in the linen closet.

History

1924 – The hotel was built by local stonemasons and owned by a stock company. It was originally named WE-GO-TA, later the name was changed to the Central Lake Hotel.

1930s – Emmons (E.B.) Gill lived in the hotel and ran it. The hotel had 22 rooms and 4 bathrooms. It also had a bar and dining room. The rooms with baths were rented for $4.50 per night and those without a bath were $2.50.

1946 – Charles A. (Art) Cronover, his wife Ruth, and Archie S. Dayton acquired the hotel.

1950s – Cliff and Etta Springstead owned the hotel.

1960s – Gary Morse purchased the hotel and renamed it The Palace. He moved the bar to the south end of the hotel and totally renovated it. The second floor was converted into living quarters for his family.

1970s – Doug and Mary Lou Denny purchased The Palace and changed the name to The Lamplight Inn. The second floor was converted into a bed and breakfast.

1986 – Ted and Betty Strezempek, along with their sons Tracy and Scott, purchased the Lamplight Inn.

1996 – The Inn was sold to Mike and Mary Ellen Murphy of Dearborn, Michigan. They changed the name to Murphy's Lamplight Inn.

2008 – Chris and Merrie Corbett purchased the Lamplight Inn and changed the name to The Blue Pelican Inn. They added the covered porch to the building and renovated the rooms, the bar, and the dining room.

Investigation

After Cliff and Etta Springstead sold the hotel in the '50s, it sat vacant for several years and fell into disrepair. It was after Gary Morse purchased it and began to do renovations that most of the haunting activity began.

Emmons B. Gill (1864-1942)

The Bride-to-be. People have seen apparitions of a young woman walking down the hallway wearing a wedding gown. A legend is told that the daughter of one of the previous hotel managers was head-over-heels in love with a local farm boy. Her father didn't approve of the relationship, so she made plans to elope. Her young fiance placed a ladder outside her bedroom window. Later that night, as she descended in her wedding dress, a piece of lace got caught in her heel, and she accidentally fell to her death. In 1979, former owner Ted Strzempek was in the upstairs hallway painting when a woman in a white wedding dress ran past him and into one of the rooms. When he inspected the room, he found it to be empty.

Mrs. Gill. During the '20s and '30s, Emmons (E.B.) Gill owned the hotel and lived there with his wife Nellie. Later they sold it, but after Emmons died in 1942, Nellie moved back into the hotel and rented there until her death in 1951. People have seen apparitions

Nellie M. Gill (1867-1951)

of Nellie in the room that used to be hers. Other times they've seen her looking out her window. On one occasion, the bar manager had closed up for the night, and, as he was leaving, he noticed someone looking out from one of the upstairs windows. He knew the room should have been empty, so he went to investigate. To his surprise he found that during the renovation the window had actually been boarded over and wasn't even accessible from inside the room.

The Happy Couple. Numerous eyewitnesses have seen an attractive couple decked out in clothing from the late '20s or early '30s. Some believe them to be E.B. and Nellie Gill, since they managed the hotel during that time period. The apparitions have been spotted dancing together near the bar. Sometimes the ghost of a little girl is seen nearby watching them. The Gills did have three daughters: Allena, Marguerita, and Merla. The youngest one may have lived at the hotel during the time her parents owned it.

The School Girl. A young girl holding her school books has been seen looking out of a second story window. Years ago, the building was used as temporary classrooms when the Central Lake School had burned down. It's also possible the apparition was Merla Gill.

Merla W. Gill (daughter of Emmons & Nellie Gill)

Whites Bridge

Location: Keene Township, Ionia County, Michigan
AKA: White's Bridge (with the apostrophe)
Coordinates: 43.01513°N 85.29913°W
Facebook: www.facebook.com/RebuildWhitesBridge

Directions: From Lowell, drive east on M-21 Bluewater Hwy. Turn left on Whites Bridge Road. Drive 5.6 miles to destination.

Ghost Lore

Sadly, the bridge is no longer there, but for several generations, the locals knew about the bridge's haunted reputation and would drive there late at night to park on the bridge and wait for the spirits to gently push them across.

- In the middle of the night, people have heard the sound of screaming coming from near the bridge.

- According to legend, a man killed his wife, children, and two friends under the bridge with a chainsaw, and his ghost haunts the bridge.

- People have heard the motor and seen the headlights of a phantom car that approaches the bridge then vanishes.

- If people drive onto the bridge, put their car in neutral, and turn off the ignition, ghosts will push their car. Afterwards, handprints can be found on the trunk. Sometimes people will first apply powder to the back of their car and later find fresh handprints.

History

1800s – The crossing of the Flat River was known as White's Crossing, named for Levi White, a prominent pioneer who settled in the area.

1840 – White erected a log and corduroy bridge to replace his earlier bridge that was crudely constructed and sagged in the middle.

1866 – White's bridge was damaged by ice jams and condemned.

1867 – It was replaced by a covered bridge built by Jared N. Brazee and J.N. Walker at a cost of $1,700. The bridge was so well constructed that it was used continuously for 146 years.

1965 – A state historical marker was installed next to the bridge.

1973 – Whites Bridge was added to The National Register of Historic Places.

2010 – A drunk driver drove through the side of the bridge.

2013 – The bridge burned and collapsed into the river. Authorities determined it was the work of arsonists. Shortly after, an Ionia County couple was convicted of stealing 300 pounds of iron fittings from charred remains at the crime scene.

Investigation

Although there's been a long history of haunting activity at the bridge, there's no evidence of a chainsaw massacre taking place there. The worst crime to occur at that location was the arson that destroyed the bridge in the summer of 2013, which left local residents devastated. Most of the people in the area have lived there for several generations, and the bridge held great sentimental meaning for them. As a family tradition, many residents had carved their names on the bridge, as did their parents, grandparents, and even their own children.

Currently, Paul Phenix, a disabled veteran from Alma, Michigan is leading the effort to rebuild the bridge. He, along with Howard Larsen, another Alma resident, founded the Rebuild Whites Covered Bridge group. Volunteers from the group and a local demolition company worked for free to remove the chunks of bridge debris from the Flat River, and an area farmer donated the fuel for the equipment. The work they did saved the county over $40,000. The group is currently seeking donations and hope to have the bridge rebuilt in the summer of 2014.

Note. Anyone with information about the fire is asked to contact the Ionia County Sheriff's Office at (616) 527-5737 or Silent Observer at (616) 527-0107.

Silent Observer is offering a $7,000 reward and I-96 Towing is offering an additional $1,000 reward for the arrest and conviction of the person or persons responsible for this act.

Ramsdell Theatre

Location: Manistee, Manistee County, Michigan
Physical Address: 101 Maple St., Manistee, MI 49660-1593
Mailing Address: P.O. Box 358, Manistee, MI 49660-0358
Phone: (231) 398-9770 (Business Office);
(231) 723-9948 (Box Office)
Email: hpefley@ramsdell-theatre.org
Website: www.ramsdelltheatre.org
Facebook: www.facebook.com/RamsdellTheatre

Ghost Lore

The town's name, Manistee, is apparently an Ojibwe term meaning "spirit of the woods." However, some of the town's residents believe the spirit might actually occupy the local Ramsdell Theatre. It was in this theatre, back in the 1950s, that a 22-year-old aspiring actor named James Earl Jones began his acting career playing Othello. After leaving Manistee, he eventually went on to collect

Tony and Emmy Awards and an Academy Award nomination. Today, he has one of the most recognizable voices in the world. In his authoritative baritone, he did the soundbite "This is CNN," voiced Mufasa in Disney's *The Lion King*, and, of course, he's the legendary voice of Darth Vader in *Star Wars*.

If that coolness factor alone isn't enough to persuade you to attend this theatre, then consider the coolness of the possibility of having a face-to-face ghostly encounter with the theatre's long-dead founder or his daughter.

- Full-bodied apparitions of T.J. Ramsdell have been seen throughout the building, sometimes floating in the air near the balcony.

- The ghost of a little girl was seen in the basement.

- The ghost of a mysterious woman was seen.

- After closing up for the night, the staff will shut off all the lights, only to return later and find the lights on.

- Doors have been known to open and close on their own.

- Light fixtures have fallen to the floor with no explanation.

History

1901 – After the two previous Manistee opera houses were destroyed by fire, T.J. Ramsdell began construction of a new theatre at a cost of over $100,000.

1903 – Construction was completed and the Ramsdell Theatre officially opened.

1909 – Ramsdell leased the theatre to the Western Theatre Association of Chicago for three years.

1917 – Ramsdell died.

1925 – The Manistee Rotarians purchased the theatre for $25,000 and turned into a movie theatre.

1939 – The building sat vacant during WWII and deteriorated.

1943 – The City of Manistee purchased the building.

1949 – The Civic Betterment Committee restored the theatre.

1953 – At the age of 22, aspiring actor James Earl Jones got his start in show business at the Ramsdell Theatre. He was initially a stage carpenter but quickly worked his way up to the position of actor and stage manager.

1972 – The theatre was listed on the National Register of Historic Places.

Investigation

Thomas Jefferson Ramsdell was a lawyer, entrepreneur, and one-term Michigan State Representative. He was born in Plymouth, Michigan in 1833, and later moved to Manistee, where at age 28 he married Nettie L. Stanton, a local school teacher. Together they had 10 children, half of whom were girls, including Nettie and Mary Antoinette, a set of twins born in 1878. Mary died at a young age and it's possible she's one of the spirits haunting the theatre. According to an article in *Traverse Magazine*, a worker at the theatre saw a little girl standing in a basement doorway. The girl looked up and uttered the cryptic message "Follow me to your fortune," then vanished. She was described as having long hair and wearing a white dress.

In 1917, Ramsdell died in Manistee at the age of 83. Surviving photos of him show him with a full head of salt-and-pepper hair and a thick white beard. He also featured a prominent nose. Staff and performers at the theatre have witnessed full-bodied apparitions of Ramsdell at various locations throughout the building. We were told that a few years ago, a series of promotional photos were shot of the interior of the theatre. One photograph of the auditorium captured the unmistakable image of T.J. Ramsdell hovering over the balcony seats.

Stafford's Perry Hotel

Location: Petoskey, Emmet County, Michigan
Address: 100 Lewis St., Petoskey, MI 49770-2449
Phone: (231) 347-4000
Reservations: 1-800-737-1899
Fax: (231) 348-6016
Email: perryhotel@staffords.com
Website: www.staffords.com
Facebook: www.facebook.com/perryhotel

Ghost Lore

At one time the town of Petoskey had over 20 competing hotels. But when Dr. Norman J. Perry constructed his hotel, he had one leg up over the competition. While the other businesses were wood structures, his was built of brick. This was in an era when people used gas lights, which tended to be a fire hazard. His hotel was billed as the only fireproof one in town. Today the only surviving hotel in town is Stafford's Perry Hotel. However, is it possible more than just the building has survived? There are some who believe in the survival of the spirit of a woman who committed suicide on the premises in 1902.

- People have seen apparitions of a woman with long, flowing hair wearing a white gown.

- The front desk has received phone calls from the hotel library—with nothing but silence on the line. The surveillance camera reveals the library to be empty.

- Guests have heard footsteps in the hallway when nobody is there.

History

1895 – Petoskey was incorporated as a city.

1899 – Dr. Norman J. Perry gave up his dental practice in Grand Rapids after the death of a patient during a multiple tooth extraction. He moved to Petoskey and built the Perry Hotel.

1919 – The hotel is purchased by Drs. John and George Reycraft with the intentions of converting it into a hospital. The city convinced them that a hotel was needed, so they maintained the hotel and built a hospital elsewhere. They hired their nephew Herbert Reycraft to manage it with his wife Hazel.

1926 – The Reycrafts doubled the capacity to 300 guests by adding a four story, 46 room wing. They doubled the hotel's capacity and added features such as a small orchestra and weekly dances.

1961 – The Reycrafts retired. The hotel was purchased by John Davis. He changed the name to the Perry-Davis Hotel. He added the panoramic window which overlooks Little Traverse Bay from the dining room.

1970s – Davis sold the hotel to Alan Gornick.

1989 – The Stafford's Hospitality company purchased the building and renovated it. They restored it to its original grandeur.

Investigation

We were able to conduct an overnight investigation in one of the guest rooms and had access to the library, restaurant, and other ghostly hotspots. The staff and manager shared several ghostly experiences that they've personally had in the hotel. Four are particularly striking.

Haunted Clock. In 1999, when the hotel was celebrating its 100 year anniversary, a housekeeper brought the manager a digital clock that was counting down backwards. The manager was unable to repair the clock and put it on a shelf where he forgot about it. Two weeks later, he noticed the clock had stopped its backwards countdown and was displaying the number 1899, which isn't even a real time, but it was the year the hotel was constructed.

Haunted Fan. One hot summer day the manager was trying to get caught up with his paperwork, when he jokingly called upon the ghost of Dr. Perry to lend a helping hand. At that moment, the box fan in the corner turned on by itself, providing him with a cool breeze as he completed his work. Later when he went to unplug it, he was startled to discover that not only had it not been turned on, but it wasn't even plugged in. He thanked Dr. Perry and quickly ran out of the office.

Lady of the Lake. There was a guest who was getting too intoxicated in the hotel's pub and was flirting with all the ladies. After retiring to bed, he awoke in the middle of the night when he felt something brush his cheek. He came face-to-face with the apparition of a woman hovering over his bed. She had long hair and was wearing a white nightgown. She shook a finger at him, as if scolding him, then pointed towards the door, which he took as a message to leave. He immediately packed his bags and checked out in the middle of the night. This ghost has been seen by others, and the hotel staff have named her "Lady of the Lake."

Haunted Chair. In November of 2005, a severe storm came across the lake. At 3:00 am strong winds blew out a window in the library on the third floor. The wind was so strong the night manager could not push open the door to the library. He had to call in the hotel manager and together they were able to pry open the door and temporarily cover the broken window with a tarp. However, the room was filled with snow and a chair sitting in front of the window was covered with broken glass. They put a closed sign on the door and left, planning to call in workmen in the morning. The night manager returned to his office and was monitoring the hotel's surveillance cameras when he saw a woman with long hair and a white night gown sitting in the library reading a book. He became concerned because the chair was covered with shards of broken glass. He called the phone in the library, but nobody answered. Running up to the library, he entered, and found the room empty. Perplexed, he returned to his office and once again saw the woman on his monitor. A second inspection of the library also found it empty. The image of the mysterious woman remained on the monitor all night and disappeared when the sun came up.

SOUTHEAST
MICHIGAN

The Witch of Seven Gables Road

Location: Dansville, Ingham County, Michigan

Directions: From Dansville head east on Dexter Trail. Turn right on Seven Gables Road (you can only turn right) and follow the road to the end where there will be a gate. The house stood a few hundred yards from where the road ends.

Ghost Lore

Many years ago, an old woman lived all alone out in the middle of nowhere. Her house sat at the end of a long wooded road. Townsfolk would often whisper to one another that the woman was an evil witch who was practicing the black arts. Curious teenagers would often venture out to her house to watch what the witch was doing. The witch became angry and bitter from the constant harassment, so before her death she placed a curse on the area that still continues to this day.

- If you let your fear overtake you and scream while on Seven Gables Road, you will die.

- Those who drive out to Seven Gables will die in a car accident within days of their visit.

- Mysterious screams can be heard coming from the woods that surrounded the old home.

History

1844 – Samuel Crossman traveled from New York and founded the town. He started a mercantile store in town and was one of the only residents.

1857 – The town was officially platted by Samuel's son, Daniel Crossman. Daniel helped out his father and eventually took over the operation of the store.

1860s – We were able to track the house back to Daniel Crossman, but it is possible that his father Samuel lived there prior to Daniel.

1867 – The town was incorporated into the Village of Dansville.

1895 – A plat book shows that several homes and roads existed near Seven Gables Road.

1940s – The home was believed to have been torn down.

Investigation

We were able to dig up several different versions of this legend. The first states that the witch cursed the fence by the gate and that if you heard a scream, it meant that next person to hop the fence would die. Another version tells of an angry mob that marched out to Seven Gables and burned down the home with the witch inside. We also found a story of a man who lived in the home with his family. Slowly the evil of the house drove the man insane. One day the man snapped and burned down the home while his family was sleeping. The man then took his own life at the end of a rope in a nearby tree.

When we began our investigation, there was quite a bit of debate among local historians as to whether the Seven Gables House even existed in Dansville. Several of the historians believed that the stories of the mysterious house amounted to nothing more than folklore and urban legend. However, as you can see from the old photo, the home did exist at one time.

It is said that the home was modeled after the Seven Gables House in Salem that inspired Nathaniel Hawthorne to write *The House of the Seven Gables*. We found no evidence that the house was ever inhabited by a witch or an insane man. However, much of the history of the home is unknown; therefore, we cannot rule out any story.

We spoke with an elderly woman who lived in Dansville her entire life. She informed us that her grandparents lived in the Seven Gables House during the late 1800s and that her father was actually born in the home. As a child the woman's father would bring her on tours of his former home. She believed that the house was not haunted and never felt anything out of the ordinary while she was at the home.

Nearly everyone in the area has heard of the legend of Seven Gables. Some older residents told us that the story has been circulating for at least 50 years.

The most common case we heard from witnesses involved mysterious screaming. Many people reported driving out to Seven Gables to see if the legend was true. While they were walking back toward where the house once stood, they would hear a loud eerie scream coming from the woods. Yet, when they tried to locate the source of the scream, nothing was ever found.

The Dare. If you are the last person from the group to jump over the fence, you will die.

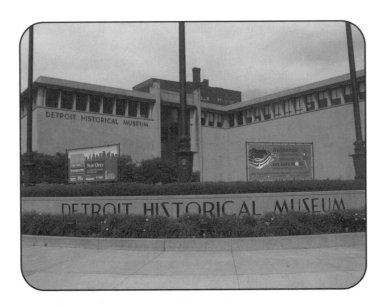

Detroit Historical Museum

Location: Detroit, Wayne County, Michigan
Address: 5401 Woodward Avenue, Detroit, MI 48202-4009
Phone: (313) 833.7935
Fax: (313) 833.5342
Email: peterp@detroithistorical.org
Website: www.detroithistorical.org

Directions: Heading west on Interstate 94 take the exit for Woodward Av. Follow Woodward to the south and the museum will be on your right.

Ghost Lore

It is widely thought that certain types of cases are more likely to produce ghosts including murders, suicides, tragic deaths, and untimely accidents. These horrific situations are believed to cause a spirit to remain in specific locations for eternity. Another newer theory on ghosts proposes that a person's spirit may become attached to an area of land, or possibly even to a treasured object. If the latter case is true, then it might help to explain the legends of the museum, because with over 200,000 items in its collection, the museum provides plenty of objects for wandering spirit to attach to.

- Mysterious orbs can be seen moving through the museum's exhibits.

- Unexplained odors plague the historic museum.

History

1921 – Clarence Burton organized 19 local historians who founded the Detroit Historical Society.

1927 – The historical society leased offices to serve as its headquarters. J. Bell Moran was given the difficult task of setting up a historical museum.

1928 – The museum opened in a one room, suite on the 23rd floor of the Barlum Tower (now the Cadillac Tower). The museum was touted as the "highest museum in the world."

1942 – *Detroit News* columnist George Stark became the president of the Detroit Historical Society.

1945 – Through the effort of Stark and others the museum had raised over $25,000. The society offered to provide the money and its 15,000 item collection to the City of Detroit on the condition that the city would agree to build and operate the historical museum.

1951 – The Detroit Historical Museum was dedicated. The ceremony was attended by numerous prominent figures including Governor G. Mennen Williams, Mayor Albert Cobo, and U.S. Senator Homer Ferguson.

1993 – The Detroit Historical Society raised over $4 million to provide an endowment fund, new exhibits, and renovations.

2006 – A formal agreement with the City of Detroit provided the Detroit Historical Society with the daily operation of the museum. Under new management the museum closed for a major makeover. The museum re-opened with several new exhibits.

Today – The museum is open to the public.

Investigation

We spoke with several staff members who informed us that many people visit the museum under the assumption that it is haunted. For years the museum's reputation as a haunted location has been growing steadily. For the most part the museum staff are tight lipped about the ghostly legends and refuse to talk about paranormal stories. Many of the workers told us that they had not had any paranormal experience at the museum.

We were unable to trace the origin of the legend back to any specific time period. It appears that while whispers of the place being haunted have been floating around for many years, the legends have increasingly gained in popularity over the last 5-10 years.

While touring the museum, many visitors have been surprised to discover strange orbs that appear in the photographs that were taken.

This case is ongoing.

The Historical Masonic Temple

Location: Detroit, Wayne County, Michigan
Address: 500 Temple Avenue, Detroit, MI 48201-2693
Phone: (313) 832-7100
Fax: (313) 832-2922
Website: www.themasonic.com

Directions: Head south on Interstate 75. Take the Mack exit to the west. Follow Mack to Cass Ave. Turn left on Cass and follow it to Charlotte and the parking lot will be on your left.

Ghost Lore

The Masonic Temple is truly a unique sight to see. With over 1,000 rooms and nearly four-million bricks used in the construction, the enormous building has plenty of space to explore. Although the Temple is located in a struggling area of Detroit surrounded by the empty remains of other elegant buildings, the Temple building still enjoys plenty of activity, both from the living and the dead.

59

- The building is filled with secret passages and secret rooms where mysterious rituals are performed.

- The building's designer became obsessed with the Temple causing his wife to leave him. Eventually the project drained his fortune and caused him to declare bankruptcy. Distraught, destitute, and alone, the man walked to the edge of the roof and jumped to his death.

- Night watchmen often encounter the spirit of the architect roaming the halls of the building he so dearly loved.

History

1891 – The Order of Detroit needed a suitable home. A committee was appointed to plan for the purchase and construction of a temple that could accommodate the Lodges, Chapters, and Council.

1892 – The first official meeting of the committee was held. The goal of the meeting was to place a value on the property which the group owned on Lafayette Boulevard. It was determined that the property was valued at $37,500. The title of the property was transferred to a new corporation that was to construct a Temple for Detroit.

1894 – The Masonic Temple Association of Detroit was formally incorporated. It was estimated that the new structure would fit the needs of the group for the next 50 years.

1896 – The various bodies moved into the new structure.

1908 – Having been in the building for only twelve years, the organization quickly grew too large for the Lafayette Boulevard Temple. The group had expanded so rapidly that a new larger building became necessary.

1913 – Plans were established to locate a larger location for a new Temple. A committee was put in charge of finding new suitable land to build the Temple. Finally, the committee decided on the land fronting on Bagg Street. George D. Mason & Company was hired to draw up the plans for the new building.

1920 – The elaborate plans for the building were completed. The enormous sum of $2,500,000 had been raised to finance the project.

1920 – Construction on the new Temple finally began. It is said that George Washington's own working tools were brought in from his Virginia Lodge to aid in the construction process.

1926 – A large ceremony celebrating the completion of the Temple took place. Thousands gathered to celebrate the grand opening.

1948 – George Mason died.

Today – Outside of official Manson meetings and business, the building is also used for a variety of community events.

Investigation

Many websites and books contain the story of George Manson's downward fall. The legend goes that George became obsessed with designing and constructing the Masonic Temple building. The process ended up draining George of his fortune, his wife, and his will to live. After filing bankruptcy, George walked up to the roof of the Temple and jumped to his death below. Now many staff and visitors report seeing his ghostly spirit wandering the halls of the building that he gave his life for.

The above tale is a great haunted story, unfortunately it not quite accurate. George Mason did design the Temple building and dedicated several years of his life to the project; however, this is where the accuracy of the popular legend stops. George Dewitt Mason died on June 3rd 1948 at the age of 91. The *Detroit Free Press* newspaper wrote in the obituary that George died at his home in the Wilshire Apartments. Although George never was depressed and suicidal, he did state that he felt like "30 cents" when quoted by the *Detroit Free Press* at a banquet held in his honor at the completion of the Temple.

Even though George did not end his life at the Temple people still are seeing the ghostly apparition of a man that is thought to be him. The spirit is most often spotted at the bottom of a staircase that leads to the roof of the building.

Through the years many employees have reported having strange experiences while inside the Temple building. The sound of doors slamming on their own is common place inside the building and with over 1000 rooms there are plenty of doors to slam.

Many times visitors to the Temple experience cold chills as they pass through certain areas of the building. We spoke with a long-time tour guide and mason who told us that many visitors to the building are overcome with a sense that they are not alone, and that the spirits of former masons still reside in the building.

Another legend of the building is that it is filled with secret rooms and passage ways used for secret mysterious rituals. Our guide took us to several of these "secret" passages and explained that once a meeting starts, no mason can officially enter through the front door, so they devised a hallway passage where late arriving masons could "sneak" in. Yet it should be noted that we did not scour the entire building and other non-public secret rooms and passages may exist.

The Whitney Restaurant

Location: Detroit, Wayne County, Michigan
Address: 4421 Woodward Avenue, Detroit, MI 48201-1821
Phone: (313) 832-5700
Email: info@thewhitney.com
Website: www.thewhitney.com

Directions: From Highway 75 turn west on Mack Avenue. Follow Mack to Woodward Avenue and turn right. The restaurant will be on your right.

Ghost Lore

If you explored the entire state of Michigan, you would have a hard time finding a restaurant more elegant than The Whitney. The fine dining establishment is known for its delicious meals served in the beautiful former estate of David Whitney. As you sit and enjoy your dining experience, engulfed by history and surrounded by antiques, you may want to keep your eyes open for the spirits that are not listed on the menu.

- Spirits inside the restaurant tend to use the elevator instead of the stairs.

- The spirit of the original owner continues to walk the floors of his home.

History

1894 – The home was constructed for David Whitney, Jr., who was a wealthy lumber baron. The 21,000-square-foot home was designed by Detroit architect Gordon W. Lloyd. The cost of the magnificent home exceeded $400,000. The family spent another $250,000 decorating the estate, and an additional $300,000 was spent on art to be displayed throughout the home.

1895 – Whitney opposed the marriage of his daughter Flora Ann, not because he disliked her husband, Mr. Rudolph Alfred Demme of Switzerland, but because, according to the newspapers, he had "a strong antipathy towards foreigners."

1900 – David Whitney, Jr. passed away in his home at the age of 70. At the time of his death, Mr. Whitney's wealth was estimated to be over 15 million dollars. After his death, Whitney's wife and family continued to reside in the family mansion.

1920s – After the family moved out, the home was used as the headquarters for the Wayne County Medical Society.

1941 – The Whitney family generously donated the mansion to the Wayne County Medical Society.

1957 – The home was sold to the Visiting Nurses Association. A $75,000 grant from the McGregor Fund helped to renovate the home to fit the needs of the association.

1972 – The home was added to the National Register of Historic Places.

1980 – The home was purchased by Richard Kughn.

1986 – The upscale Whitney Restaurant opened for business.

2007 – Mr. Kughn sold the property to Mr. Bud Liebler.

2008 – The third floor "Ghost Bar" opened at the restaurant.

2008 – The restaurant hosted the event "History, Mystery, and Haunting: The Whitney," which gave guests a chance to participate in an investigation while enjoying a dinner.

Today – The restaurant is open to the public.

Investigation

Legend states that both Mr. Whitney and his wife Sara died in the family home. It is believed that their spirits continue to haunt their former residence. Our investigation found that Mr. Whitney did indeed die in his home as reported on November 29th, 1900 by the *New York Times* newspaper.

It is the wandering spirit of a man believed to be Mr. Whitney that has been spotted walking around on the second and third floors of the restaurant. If it is the spirit of Mr. Whitney, the owners told us that they believe he is a friendly spirit who simply loves his former home and has never caused any real problems.

Many of the reported paranormal events revolve around the restaurant's elevator. Witnesses have seen the elevator operating on its own while moving up and down between floors, even though it is completely empty. In order to determine what might be causing these odd elevator malfunctions, maintenance repair workers have been called in to diagnose the situation. However, after completing a thorough investigation of the elevator, no cause for the weird actions can be located and the mysterious elevator actions resume.

On the third floor sits the upscale "Ghost Bar." The bar was added to provide the city with a new classy, relaxed hangout. It is in this newly renovated room that a lot of the paranormal activity takes place. Many staff believe that the area of the Ghost Bar is the most haunted room in the entire restaurant.

Those working late at the restaurant have often heard the sounds of the restaurant's piano being played. Knowing that no one else should be in the restaurant, the curious witnesses will venture over to the piano only to see that it is playing all by itself.

Puttygut Bridge

Location: East China, Saint Clair County, Michigan
Address: Puttygut Road, East China, MI 48054

Directions: From Interstate 94 turn south on Palms Road. Turn left on Puttygut Road (30 Mile Road). It will be a dirt road. Follow it to the bridge. The bridge is just east of Mayer Road.

Ghost Lore

One evening, a local man had consumed a few too many beers at his favorite watering hole. The highly intoxicated man unwisely decided that he was sober enough to safely drive his truck back to his home. While en route to his house, the drunken man lost control of the truck and crashed over the side of Puttygut Bridge, into the flooded water below. When it was discovered that the man never made it home, the neighbors searched the bridge and surrounding area for him, but no one ever found the man or his truck. His spirit now sits out on Puttygut Bridge, patiently waiting for visitors.

- A disembodied light can be seen floating through the area of the bridge.

- Late at night the phantom sounds of a truck crashing into the water can be heard from the bridge. After hearing the splashing noise, the man will appear in front of you.

History

1904 – A wood plank bridge was constructed on Puttygut Road.

1968 – The original bridge was fitted with a new deck. The deck is the part of the bridge that you drive over, and it was replaced with new wood planks.

1992 – The current concrete bridge was constructed.

Investigation

We were unable to locate any records of a person crashing their vehicle on Puttygut Bridge. In addition, the relatively shallow stream that runs beneath the bridge would make it nearly impossible to hide a full size truck. We spoke with both the Sheriff's Department and the Saint Clair County Road Commission, and neither organization had taken a report of a truck crashing out on Putttygut Road.

This case gets even more convoluted due to the fact that the legend has no date or time period associated with it, making it much more difficult to determine if a crash ever really took place.

One group of skeptics headed out to the bridge to discover for themselves if the legend was true. When they got to the bridge they noticed a bright round light slightly off in the distance. As the group observed the light for a few moments, they could not figure out where the light was coming from. They became very curious and decided to drive down to further check out the light. However, once they got to where the light had been spotted, they could find no explanation for the light.

The rural bridge does seem to be a popular destination, as evidenced by the liberal amount of graffiti and writing on its walls. We spoke with several residents of the area who had all heard stories of people having paranormal experiences while out on the bridge. One young man we spoke with claimed that one night he drove out to the bridge with a couple of his friends to debunk the legend. However, once the group arrived at the bridge, they were so spooked that they did not stick around to investigate.

The Dare. If you drive out to the bridge, stop your car, and set your keys on your roof, the spirit of the drunk man will appear in front of you.

First State Bank

Location: Eastpointe, Macomb County, Michigan
Address: 15000 East Ten Mile Road, Eastpointe,MI 48021-1001
Phone: (586) 775-5000
Fax: (586) 445-6646

Directions: From Hwy. 97 turn east on E. 10 Mile Rd. Follow the road until you pass Hayes Blvd. and the bank will be on your right side.

Ghost Lore

When you think of haunted places, banks may not be the first places that pop into your head. That is because most people do not think of banks as inherently haunted places. However, the First State Bank in Eastpointe might just change the way in which you view banks, because during the 1940s a young teller was shot to death during a robbery. Ever since that fateful day, bank patrons have seen the restless spirit of the young teller throughout the bank.

- Late at night the spirit of a murdered bank teller haunts the drive-thru.

- A shadowy image of a man is often seen peeking out of the bank windows and pointing at those who pass by.

History

1917 – The Halfway State Bank first opened its doors on the corner of 9 Mile and Gratiot in the Village of Halfway (now Eastpointe). Two other locations soon opened as well.

1929 – The name of the Halfway State Bank was changed to First State Bank.

Today – The bank is open for business.

Investigation

We spoke with several long time staff members of the bank who informed us that the bank receives a lot of inquiries about the haunted legend. However, the staff assured us that, to the best of their research, no employee had ever been killed in the bank. The employees were not sure how or when this legend originated.

The police chief told us that the police station does not have any records dating back to the 1940s, as the police station was not constructed until the late 1950s and was finally dedicated in 1960.

Many witnesses claim to have seen the faint image of a man inside the drive-thru window. At first it appears that the man is just simply a night maintenance worker going about his job. It is not until the man disappears right before their eyes that the witnesses conclude that he is not a living employee. This investigation is still ongoing.

The Dare. If you pull into the bank near the ATM machine late at night, shut off your lights and look into the drive-thru window, you will see the ghost of the murdered young teller pointing his finger directly at you.

Fenton Hotel

Location: Fenton, Genesee County, Michigan
Address: 302 North Leroy Street, Fenton, MI 48430-2730
Phone: (810) 750-9463
Fax: (810) 750-9461
Email: nsorise@comcast.net
Website: www.fentonhotel.com

Directions: From Silver Lake Rd. turn north onto N. Leroy St. and follow it to the hotel.

Ghost Lore

The Historic Fenton Hotel has dutifully served the community for over 150 years. Although the business no longer offers lodging to weary travelers, the beautifully restored restaurant still provides a central gathering place where both locals and travelers feel at ease. You will not have to look hard in order to find the legends of this place, as the haunted history is listed right on the menu.

73

...ime hotel caretaker refuses to let death stop him from ...; after the building.

- A mysterious spirit has a habit of ordering whiskey and then disappearing.

- Many rooms were rented by women who were employed at nearby houses of ill repute. One former working girl now haunts that area where she took her own life.

- An unknown man appears throughout the building wearing an old top hat and long black coat.

History

1856 – The Vermont House was constructed. Mr. Seed served as the property's first landlord.

1868 – The hotel's name was changed to the Fenton House. Abner Roberts served as the proprietor of the hotel.

1882 – The hotel was purchased by D. W. DeNio. The hotel was renamed the "DeNio House." Mr. DeNio set about renovating the entire building, complete with new expensive furnishings. To celebrate the extensive renovation a grand opening celebration was held. Hosted by the Carpediem Club, over 200 of the town's finest guests attended the lavish soiree.

1883 – The DeNio Hotel was one of the first buildings in town to install a telephone line.

1886 – The first floor of the building, which contained the billiard room, bar, and sample room, was renovated.

1898 – The hotel was renamed "The Fenton House" under the proprietorship of Mr. Hurd. Mr. Hurd also constructed a new brick kitchen, installed a new stream heating plant, and made improvements to the employees' quarters on the second floor.

1904 – The second and third floor porches were knocked down when John Moyer's team of horses got spooked and ran, knocking out the porch's supporting posts.

1916 – The hotel was purchased by T. J. Dumanois. Mr. Dumanois also owned the Linden Hotel.

1930s – During the Great Depression, the hotel temporary closed.

1933 – After the repeal of Prohibition, the hotel reopened. The hotel was managed by Arthur Dumanois (The son of T. J.) and his wife Margaret. Legend states that the Fenton Hotel was issued the first post-Prohibition liquor license in Genesee County.

1930s to 1940s – The hotel began a slow move away from lodging and was used mostly as a restaurant.

1946 – The business was purchased by Ray & A O'Reilly. The name was changed to "Hotel Fenton."

1970s to 1990s – During this time the business changed hands numerous times.

1980 – The building was placed on the National Register of Historic Places.

1997 – Nick and Peggy Sorise purchased the Fenton Hotel.

2006 – The hotel celebrated 150 years of business. The name was officially changed to the "Fenton Hotel Tavern & Grille."

Source: Fenton Hotel Tavern & Grille

Investigation

The owner told us about one of the main legends of the hotel. Years back a young woman was working as a server when she fell head over heels in love with a traveling salesman. A short romance brewed until the woman discovered she was pregnant. Upon hearing the news, the salesman said he wanted nothing to do with the woman and skipped town without delay. She became so distraught at the though of being an unwed mother that she hanged herself outside the second floor window.

It is the spirit of this deceased server that is one of the ghosts thought to be haunting the establishment. Her spirit is now most often seen, heard, and felt inside the women's bathroom. The owner stated that over the last five years three different people have had a weird experience with a spirit while in the third stall of the women's restroom. One customer claimed to have had her hair lightly pulled from some unseen force.

In her book, *Weird Michigan*, Linda Godfrey writes that one of the resident ghosts is that of a long-time caretaker named Emery. While alive, Emery enjoyed the comforts of his upstairs lodging. Even though Emery has long since passed, his footsteps can be clearly heard rattling the building's tin ceiling as he paces back and forth near his old third floor dwelling.

Staff members claim that on numerous occasions, while closing up for the evening, they have heard unexplained pounding and thumping coming from the area of Emery's old room. Workers believe that it is simply Emery's subtle way of encouraging them to hurry up and finish so he can finally get some rest for the night.

It appears that the restaurant is also home to a ghost with a fondness for whiskey. On several occasions a nicely dressed man seated at a table has ordered a glass of Jack Daniels whiskey on the rocks. However, when the drink is served, the man is nowhere to be found.

In *Haunted Michigan*, author Gerald Hunter tells of a young woman who was going into the back storage area in order to grab some liquor bottles for the bar. After securing the liquor the woman turned around to head back and was startled by the appearance of a man in a top hat and black coat staring at her from the doorway. The woman immediately knew the man was a ghost as he appeared in black and white.

Evergreen Cemetery

Location: Grand Blanc, Genesee County, Michigan
Address: 3415 East Hill Road, Grand Blanc, MI 48439-8106
Phone: (810) 694-6541

Directions: From Highway 54 south turn left onto E. Hill Road and follow it over the railroad tracks. The cemetery will be on your left.

Ghost Lore

At first glance nothing looks out of the ordinary at the Evergreen Cemetery. Like most cemeteries, Evergreen is neatly kept and stocked full of grave markers, flowers, and family memories. Yet, if you deepen your investigation, you will see that this "ordinary" cemetery is also home to bizarre shadows, disembodied lights, and chanting robed figures.

- In the back of the cemetery there is a section of graves where no adults are allowed burial.

- At night you can see unknown shadows stealthily moving throughout the cemetery.

History

1840s – Jonathan Davison leased six acres of land to be used for the Evergreen Cemetery. The lease agreement was established for 99 years.

1859 – The Evergreen Cemetery Association held their first meeting.

1873 – The area was listed as Gibsonville in the *Atlas of Genesee County, Michigan.* It was named after C. D. W. Gibson. The railroad tracks run west of the cemetery due to the fact that Mr. Gibson would not grant the railroad permission to cross his property.

1879 – Mr. Gibson's decision to spurn the railroad slowly forced business to Grand Blanc, and the area of Gibsonville became known as Whigville.

1950s – Jonathan Davison's original lease agreement expired. The land was transferred to the cemetery.

Source: Grand Blanc Heritage Association

Investigation

In the back of the cemetery there is a unique section of graves called "Babyland." This area is filled with the graves of young children and infants. Loved ones routinely bring toys and assorted stuffed animals to decorate the graves.

The cemetery superintendent was working one evening when he noticed some weird lights flickering next to a far off grave. As he started walking toward the lights, he noticed that they were coming from a group of robed figures holding candles. The man thought he heard chanting and it looked like the group was performing some type of ritual. As the man crept closer, the robed figures finally noticed him and disappeared into the darkness of the night.

Many of the staff have heard unexplained sounds coming from inside the cemetery. The most commonly reported odd noise is that of phantom footsteps moving throughout the cemetery. Intrigued by the mysterious footsteps, visitors and staff often try to locate the cause of the noise, yet no source is ever found and the footsteps simply stop.

A long time employee of the cemetery told us that over the years she has personally witnessed several unexplained events. She stated that while sitting at her desk working, she would often hear the door chimes ring as though someone had just opened the front door. Yet, much to her surprise, every time she looked up, no one was standing there and the door was completely closed. The woman also reported that on many occasions she had spotted strange, dark shadows moving around the building and the cemetery. She believed that, in addition to the cemetery, the main office was haunted as well.

For years reports of mysterious shadows have been plaguing the cemetery. A staff member told us that his co-workers would often spot these unknown shadows floating throughout the cemetery. All attempts to track these shadows have failed.

Several different ghost hunting groups have set up investigations in the cemetery to try to explain the mystery. The groups have found that several strange mists and orbs have appeared in their film.

Holly Hotel

Location: Holly, Oakland County, Michigan
Address: The Historic Holly Hotel,
110 Battle Alley, Holly, MI 48442-1608
Phone: (248) 634-5208
Website: www.hollyhotel.com

Directions: Take E. Maple St. to the west and turn left on
Alley Street. Go down to the end of the block and the Holly
Hotel will be on your right.

Ghost Lore

From the moment you step through the doors of the Holly Hotel
you feel like you have been transported back in time 100 years.
The overwhelming beauty of the place is only enhanced by its
history that is tactfully plastered all over the walls. Suddenly it is
easy to imagine the place filled with noisy railroad employees,

81

well-dressed traveling lumber barons, and colorful locals all sitting around smoking cigars and drinking whiskey while hashing over the important news of the day. It is only when the staff welcome you that you slowly return to today's world. Having investigated hundreds of places with ghostly legends, we are always prepared for a myriad of reactions from the staff when asked about the paranormal activity. However, when we spoke with the staff at the Holly Hotel we were quite surprised at just how casually they embraced the hotel's haunted reputation. I guess that if you spent your time around ghostly activity and constantly heard stories of people's experiences you might be a bit casual, too. Or maybe you wouldn't. There is only one way for you to find out.

- At night the mysterious sounds of a phantom game of billiards being played echo throughout the building.

- The cigar-smoking spirit of the original former owner still walks the halls of the restaurant dressed in clothing from a long forgotten era.

History

1863 – The two-story wooden Washington House building occupied the land on the corner where the Holly Hotel now rests. Due to the numerous trains that steamed through city, the hotel served as a popular hangout for railroad employees, transients, and a variety of other unsavory characters. The area quickly gained a seedy reputation as a place were violence ruled, and so many fights erupted in the alley that it garnered the name "Battle Alley."

1891 – A new building was constructed. The three-story red brick building was erected in a Queen Anne style. The first proprietor of the establishment was Mr. John Hirst.

1900s – The hotel was a hotbed of activity. Many local and regional civil and social groups descended upon the hotel for their meetings and annual gatherings.

1908 – Under the Pro-temperance league, Carry A. Nation and her supporters came to the hotel to spread their message about the evils of drinking. Much to his credit the owner of the hotel refused to condemn those who were partaking in the hotel's finer beverages. The temperance group was so dedicated to the cause that they used their umbrellas to club those patrons who were enjoying drinks in the hotel. Mrs. Nation also brought in her axe to break bottles and intimidate customers. Finally, when Mrs. Nation's actions were too much to put up with, she was arrested and thrown in jail, an act that would cause Governor Warner to visit the town.

1912 – The building was purchased by Joseph P. Allen of New York. Mr. Allen renamed the business Holly Inn.

1913 – A considerable fire engulfed the building and destroyed the second and third floors. Immediately after the fire, Mr. Allen began building a newer and better designed hotel. The new hotel was christened the "Allendorf Hotel," in an attempt to imitate the world renowned Waldorf Hotel in New York.

1930s to 60s – The hotel, along with many other businesses in Holly, fell into a state of disrepair. The once proud hotel was now known as a popular rundown boarding house for transients. The hotel restaurant had fallen just as far, and was mainly known for serving standard pizza and beer.

1978 – The hotel was hit by another fire. The blaze swept through the building causing an estimated $550,000 worth of damage to the hotel. Four people living at the hotel were injured in the fire. Investigators blamed the fire on arson.

1978 – An ambitious renovation began with the goal of restoring the hotel to its original grandeur. In order to accurately reconstruct the hotel, drawings from the hotel as it was in 1891 were used in conjunction with eye witness memory from local historians.

1980 – The property was added to the National Register of Historic Places.

Today – The Hotel is operated as a restaurant and is open to the public.

Source: Holly Hotel

Investigation

There is so much paranormal activity happening at the hotel that you could easily fill an entire book with the bizarre stories. Unfortunately, space prohibits us from covering all of them, but these examples should get you started.

In 1989, Professor Norman Gauthier conducted an investigation of the restaurant. When the investigation was complete, Gauthier was convinced that the place was loaded with spirits. The restaurant staff also told us that they too believe that the place is haunted by several ghosts, yet two of the spirits seem to be the most active.

Mr. Hirst. It was said that the Holly Hotel's original owner, Mr. Hirst, truly enjoyed the comforts of a quality cigar. Even through Mr. Hirst passed away in the 1920s, the scent of his cigar can still be perceived today. Many guests are overcome with the scent of a cigar being consumed, however no cause of the fragrance can be detected and it is believed that the odor is coming from the spirit of Mr. Hirst who continues his unhealthy habit.

The spirit of Mr. Hirst does not end with cigar smoke, as many guests and staff have seen the foggy apparition of a man thought to be Mr. Hirst pass through the restaurant. Witnesses claim the man is nicely dressed in a frock and top hat. Mr. Hirst has even been known to talk. On occasion the disembodied voice of a man can be heard by guests. Although the voice can be clearly heard, the garbled words remain undecipherable.

Nora Kane. A portrait of Nora Kane hangs on the wall of the main lobby. However, numerous visitors to the hotel believe the spirit of Nora has appeared in many of the photos taken inside the hotel.

It is said that while Nora was alive she was a lover of music and could often be heard treating patrons to a beautiful song on the piano. Today, guests are still treated to the musical talents of Nora as on quiet nights the sound of beautiful music periodically drifts through the building. Those lucky enough to hear the supernatural notes believe that Nora is gracing their presence with another lovely song.

Nora also seems to hold a special fondness for the bar. It is here that unsuspecting visitors have caught the scent of women's perfume passing by. Curious to see who is wearing so much perfume the visitors glance over their shoulder only to see that no one has passed by them.

Other Paranormal Activity. During the 1940s, the hotel housed a billiards table to entertain its guests. However, those days are over and a pool table has not occupied the hotel for many years. Today many people hold their wedding celebrations upstairs at the hotel. While enjoying the celebration that is going on upstairs, guests report hearing the sounds of billiards balls been struck against one another. The pool game sounds ring so clear that guests often inquire with the staff about being able to play a game. Each time the odd request has been made the guest is told that the hotel doesn't have a billiards table, and that what they heard were the phantom sounds of a game played long ago.

We spoke with several bartenders who told us that unexplainable events are not uncommon in the bar. On many nights, the bartenders have witnessed full bottles of liquor move across the bar on their own. Chairs in the bar also have been seen sliding across the floor as if pushed by a pair of undetectable hands.

Union Chapel Cemetery

Location: Inkster, Wayne County, Michigan
Address: 27042 Michigan Avenue, Inkster, MI 48141

Directions: This cemetery is very difficult to spot from the road. Take Michigan Avenue (Hwy. 12) to the west. Once you pass Inkster Road, slow down and you will see the St. Vincent de Paul thrift store on your right (27114 Michigan Avenue). The cemetery is right across the street on your left side.

Mary's Grave: The grave is located in the left corner of the cemetery and her gravestone is placed flat against the ground.

Ghost Lore

Along the hustle and bustle of Michigan Avenue is a small secluded graveyard that quietly sits back off the main road easily hidden from the eyes of passing motorists. It is here that those who are fortunate enough to find the historic cemetery encounter the roaming spirit of a young girl who is buried there.

- The ghost of a little girl will appear in photos taken of her grave.

- Those who visit the cemetery hear the faint unexplained sound of a young girl talking.

History

1825 – James Wightman purchased the west half of section 30, which totaled 80 acres. The land was in the district of Detroit and Territory of Michigan.

1827 – Wightman sold 40 acres of his land to his son Hiram Wightman.

1833 – Francis Ruff purchased all parts of the east half and half of the west portion of land of section 30. An unofficial cemetery was established. It was originally referred to as the "burying ground." Researchers believe that the name of Union Chapel Cemetery came from the consolidation of a Methodist and Episcopal church that operated in the area.

1855 – Francis and his wife Polly sold part of their land to David Ruff to be used for the sole purpose of a burying ground.

1860s – A total of 46 lots were platted and sold. The price for each lot was $7.00, which also included a burial right certificate.

1862 – A church called the Nankin-Dearborn Townline Methodist Episcopal Church was completed. The church sat across the road from the cemetery.

1866 – Mary Jane Walker died. She was nine years old at the time of her death.

1871 – 1873 Several deeds show that Francis continued to sell burial lots inside of Union Chapel.

1877 – Records listed the cemetery stockholders, their lot numbers, and whether or not they had paid their annual $1.80 assessment fee.

1906 – An additional piece of land was purchased for the cemetery by Anthony Weithoff. This was the last piece of land that would be purchased for the cemetery.

1925 – The Nankin-Dearborn Townline Methodist Episcopal Church was destroyed by fire.

Source: Lisa Carter, *Historic Preservation and Planning,* 2007, Eastern Michigan University.

Investigation

Little is known about the origin of this strange legend. We were unable to determine how or when the legend began. What we do know is that the legend states that there is a young girl buried in the cemetery, and if you locate her grave all sorts of weird things will happen to you and to your pictures. We discovered that there are several young women buried throughout the cemetery. However, the legend only involves the grave of a young girl named Mary Jane Walker. Mary was only nine years of age when she died in 1866.

Several curious legend trippers have reported having strange orbs and a fog-like substance appear in the photographs that were taken at Mary's grave.

We were told by several groups of researchers that when they took audio recorders with them to Mary's grave, they captured the voice of a young girl talking to them. The researchers believed that the baffling voice was that of Mary Jane Walker.

The Dare. If you locate the grave of the young Mary Jane Walker, you must ask for her permission to take a picture. If you do, she will make herself appear on your photo.

A Ghostly Family Reunion at the Crouch–Reynolds Cemetery

Location: Jackson, Jackson County, Michigan

Directions: Corner of Reynolds Rd. and Horton Dr. Take Highway 60 (Spring Arbor Road) to the west and turn left on Reynolds Rd. Follow it to the corner of Horton Dr. and the cemetery will be right there.

Jacob's Grave: The unmarked grave is located just to the right of the main gate under the spirea bush.

Ghost Lore

Every year a father and his loving daughter reunite in a small rural cemetery in the middle of nowhere. Neighbors report that this family rendezvous has been occurring for quite some time. Their annual meeting is not too inconvenient, as the father doesn't have far to travel and his daughter is located less than five miles away. The only thing that makes this case odd is the fact that both the father and daughter have been dead for over 100 years.

- Mysterious mist floats down Reynolds Rd. and disappears once it gets to a certain unmarked grave.

- On one specific night each year, the spirits of a murdered father and daughter come together inside the graveyard.

History

1883 –   Jacob Crouch, Henry and Eunice White, and Moses Polley were shot to death in their sleep.

Investigation

Here is the scenario that the investigators put together after the murders. Sometime during the evening of November 21st and morning of November 22nd, 1883 someone entered the Crouch farm and brutally shot four people as they were sleeping. The case was never solved.

Victims

Jacob Crouch. Jacob was seventy-four years old and one of the wealthiest farmers in Michigan. Four years prior to his death, he purchased a 15,000-acre ranch in Texas that was said to be worth over $1 million. It was believed that Jacob had just received a huge sum of money from his Texas ranch profits. Jacob was shot in the left side of the head behind his ear and once in the neck. According to the *Galveston Daily News*, Jacob was the only victim that seemed to put up a struggle.

Eunice White (Jacob's Daughter). Eunice was in the final stages of her pregnancy when she was shot five times while attempting to escape. Eunice was shot twice in the right arm, once in her right wrist, once through her lungs, and once in her lower jaw.

Henry White (Eunice's Husband). Henry was shot twice. One shot struck an artery in the right side of his head, while the other shot entered his right temple near his eye.

Moses Polley (A Visitor). Moses was a Pennsylvania cattleman who had traveled to Michigan to conduct some business with Jacob. Mr. Polley was found with a hole in the back of his neck.

Non-Victims

Julie Reese (A domestic). Julie claimed that she had slept through the whole affair. Her room was only 25 feet away from the shootings.

George Boles (A young servant). George first claimed that he knew nothing of the deaths. George later changed his story, and stated that after hearing what sounded like gunfire, he jumped into a nearby chest and hid there all night. However, the chest that George claimed to have hidden in was found to be too small for him to fit into. George was held by police, but was eventually released.

Clues

Gun. Investigators found several empty cartridges on the floor indicating that the murderer had reloaded his weapon. All of the balls were the same size, leading to the conclusion that only one weapon was used in the murders.

Tracks Outside. Investigators found tracks outside in the snow leading them to believe that someone may have stood guard while the murders were taking place inside the home.

Chloroform. *The Janesville Daily Gazette* newspaper reported that once the word of the killings got out, curious neighbors who rushed to the house smelled a strong scent of chloroform in the air, raising the theory that some of the victims may have been chloroformed before being shot. However, several doctors reported that no chloroform was used.

Theories

Two Men. Jud Crouch (Jacob's Son) and Dan Holcomb (Jacob's Son-in-law) were arrested and held for the murders. It is thought that the two men committed the crime for the money. Both men were charged with the murders, but both were found innocent by a jury.

Railroad Passengers. One of the most credible theories is that on his way to Michigan, Mr. Polley bragged about his wealth and perhaps even flashed a lot of money around the train. This type of behavior attracted some of the less-desirable characters who then followed him to Jacob's and attempted to rob him and Jacob.

Paranormal Activity

Surprisingly, the haunted activity does not happen at the old farm site of Jacob Crouch. Instead, the strange happenings take place in the cemetery where Jacob Crouch is buried.

The main version of the legend is that each year on the anniversary of the murders, the spirit of Eunice White rises up from her grave in St. John Catholic Cemetery and travels to Crouch-Reynolds Cemetery to once again be reunited with her father.

It is said that shortly after the murders took place, witnesses began seeing a ghostly white mist appearing over the grave of Jacob. Those who saw the anomaly believed that the mist was the disembodied spirit of Eunice trying to be close to her father. Many of the witnesses claim that the mist or fog will disappear once it reaches Jacob's grave.

The Dare. If you visit the graveyard on the evening of November 21st, you will encounter the ghost of Jacob Crouch and his daughter Eunice.

Linden Hotel

Location: Linden, Genesee County, Michigan
Address: 122 East Broad Street, Linden, MI 48451-9126
Phone: (810) 735-5780
Website: www.lindenhotel.com

Ghost Lore

Throughout the country there are some long-running businesses that have beaten the odds and found a way to survive through competition, recessions, and even the Great Depression. Many of these historic places embrace their long history and enjoy the feeling of being established long before any of us were born. The Linden Hotel is one such historic place. Although no longer a hotel, the restaurant prides itself on having served the community for over 150 years. Like most historic places, the Linden Hotel embraces its history and all of the stories and events that go along with it. However, unlike most other restaurants, after eating at the

Linden Hotel you may want to check your backseat to ensure you don't bring home more than just your unfinished food.

- The apparition of an unknown soldier often appears in photographs taken at the restaurant.

- Doors mysteriously open and close on their own.

- The spirit of a young girl follows customers home.

History

1840 – The hotel was constructed by Warner and Harris. The owners harvested the necessary timber from woods near Alonzo Chapin's land. It was known throughout the area as "The Exchange." The hotel was owned by Ed Dumanois.

1850 – Seth C. Sadler owned the building and began rebuilding and renovating the property.

1887 to 1900 – Once again the building was in need of repairs. William Gamber began another renovation of the building.

1921 – The hotel was sold to James and Emma Reip. The couple decided to change the name of the hotel to the "House of Plenty."

1954 – After sitting on one location for over 100 years, the House of Plenty was moved. The entire building was swung around from the corner of East Broad Street and Bridge Street to face East Broad Street, the location where it rests today.

1993 – The establishment was purchased by Jack and Rose Furry.

Today – The restaurant is operated by the Furry's three children: Mike, Sharon and Karen.

Investigation

We spoke with one of the owners who informed us that the business has not always had a haunted reputation. We were told that the majority of unusual activity started in the late 1990s, or at least that is when people started to talk about it.

Both visitors and staff have reported seeing and hearing the doors in the restaurant opening and closing on their own, as though they had been guided by some unseen force.

One day, an outside contractor was called in to do some minor repairs in the restaurant. As the man was working, he clearly heard the voice of a man telling him to have some whiskey. The confused worker glanced around to see who was talking to him, but he quickly discovered the place was completely empty.

While enjoying a nice meal in the restaurant, a woman reported seeing the ghostly image of a man walking through the dining area. What made this sighting so bizarre is the fact that the man appeared to be wearing an old pair of overalls and looked like he was an old farmer from a time long since past.

Many of the staff have reported hearing the sound of a baby crying upstairs. It is reported that a local ABC TV station from Flint captured the puzzling sound on tape.

The baby crying is not the only odd noise to come from the restaurant, as employees often hear the phantom sounds of people walking around the upstairs storage area. However, after hearing repeated occurrences of unknown footsteps, a search of the storage area was finally made and no one was found.

One evening a woman and her young daughter finished their meal, left the restaurant and headed for home. A few minutes later the mother came back to the restaurant with a bizarre story. While the family was driving home, the young girl kept talking to someone in the backseat. The curious mother inquired about the conversation and the young girl informed her that she was talking to the nice woman from the restaurant who was coming home with them. The mother hoped that if she returned to the restaurant, the ghost would stay there as well. The mother was certainly not alone in her experience, as several patrons have stated that they too brought a spirit home with them.

During one of the town's Civil War re-enactments, several photographs of the participants were taken inside the restaurant. When the photos were developed the staff noticed the hazy image of an unknown man standing in the room. The "man" was apparent in all the photos that were taken. No one recalled seeing the mysterious soldier when the photo was taken and no one was able to recognize who it was. If you are looking to analyze the unknown soldier for yourself, you can view all of the strange photos at the restaurant.

Camp Lady by the Lake

Location: Luna Pier, Monroe County, Michigan
Address: Luna Pier, MI 48157

Directions: From Luna Pier take Interstate 75 south to exit 5 (Erie Rd.). Turn left on the road and follow it to the fence. You will have to park your vehicle here and walk the rest of the way. Just before you get to the lake you will see a path on your left. This area was where the camp rested.

Ghost Lore

Many years ago, a woman managed a summer camp for orphans. One morning, the woman went out for a leisurely walk along the beach. While she was gone, a terrible fire rushed through the camp burning all of the children to death. By the time the woman returned all that was left of the camp was the charred bodies of the children. The woman was overcome with guilt and blamed herself for all of the dead children. In fact, she was so distraught by the horrible death the children suffered that she took her own life.

- At night, the dead children rise up and can be seen playing throughout the remains of the camp.

- A woman's watchful spirit eternally patrols the area protecting the camp from any danger.

History

1953 – The Consumer Power Company began operations near the water.

1954 – The Camp Lady of the Lake officially opened. It was established by Msgr. Michael J. Doyle and headed by the Toledo Catholic Charities Incorporated out of Toledo.

1960s – It is believed that the camp closed down during this time period.

1970 – A group of immigrant workers petitioned to have a living camp site at the former Camp Lady of the Lake.

2008 – The *Monroe News* newspaper reported that the camp area was added to the Detroit River International Wildlife Refuge.

Investigation

It is an understatement that the real history of the Camp Lady of the Lake is hard to find. Nearly everyone we spoke with was familiar with the haunted legends, yet no one had any information on the history of the camp.

Skeptics claim that the whole legend was created by writer Linda M. Fields who wrote a fictional story titled "Our Lady Of The Lake." Linda told us that her story is indeed fiction, but inspired by the real camp.

Our investigation showed that there was a Catholic camp called Camp Lady of the Lake that opened in 1954. According to the May 27th, 1954 edition of *Mansfield News Journal* (Ohio), the camp was open to both the boys and girls of Toledo area. The camp was operated by the Toledo Catholic Charities Inc., and was a Catholic summer camp. The camp was established by Msgr. Michael J. Doyle and was run by the Sisters of the church.

The camp was open to boys between the ages of 7 and 13 and girls between 7 and 15. The campers lived in small individual cabins, and the activities were listed as water sports, arts, crafts, games, nature hikes, music, and campfires. The 1954 article does not specify that the children needed to be orphans in order to attend the camp. However, a July 8th, 1970 article in the *Independent Newspaper* out of California stated that the closed camp had been used for Toledo area orphans.

We are unsure as to the exact date of the camp's closing. We found a story from 1960 that stated the camp was hosting a meeting titled "Day of Recollection for Catholic girls in Scouting." The 1970 article claimed that the camp had gone mostly unused for several years, which would put the closing of the camp sometime in the mid 1960s. During that time a group of immigrant workers were camped out in the area and were seeking permission to remain living in the area. It is believed that the original camp closed down due to constant flooding that ravaged the area. The church did not have the necessary funds to continually repair the structures so they left the camp unused. We were unable to find any stories of the camp burning down or of a woman committing suicide there.

It seems that much of the paranormal activity takes place late at night. Several local residents told us that they had heard warnings that you should not go out to the camp at night because of all the odd and mysterious things that place there.

Linda Godfrey, on her website Weird Michigan, collected a story from a young girl who tagged along with some friends as they headed out to the camp at 2:00 am. When the group first arrived they began hearing some sort of sinister laughing coming from the woods, but they shrugged it off, thinking it was only their imagination. A few moments later, the young woman saw the ghost of a little girl standing in front of her. The girl was wearing an old dress and was surrounded by a glowing white light. Startled by the appearance of the little girl the group immediately took off running for their car. While they were running, the young woman felt as though she was pushed in her back by some unseen force behind her.

Numerous legend trippers have gone to the camp late at night and were overwhelmed with the creepy feeling that they were certainly not alone out there. It is very common for visitors to return from the camp with mysterious orbs and unknown lights appearing in their pictures.

The Dare. If you visit the camp at night, you will encounter the ghost of the woman who killed herself.

Red Apple Inn

Location: Wayne, Wayne County, Michigan
Address: Wayne's Red Apple Inn, 32711 Michigan Avenue,
Wayne, MI 48184-1430
Phone: (734) 722-4100

Directions: The Inn and restaurant are located right in the
middle of town on Michigan Ave., which is also Highway 12.

Ghost Lore

Motels are not inherently scary places, but thanks to movies like
Psycho, Vacancy, and *Hostel,* Hollywood has created the fear of
spending the night in an unknown place. As kids, we all heard and
even told the terrible tales of death and dismemberment that take
place in secluded motels. In most cases these wild stories are
nothing more than standard urban legends circulated by teenagers
and perhaps Holiday Inn executives. However, in Wayne the Red

Apple Inn has gained a dark reputation for being haunted due to many cases of tragedy and death that have taken place there. Even though no one has been killed inside the motel, you may want to watch out if you plan to eat pizza or consummate your wedding at the motel.

- A man stabbed to death in his room plays tricks on unsuspecting guests.

- Soap, shampoo, and even the TV remote go missing inside the hotel's haunted rooms.

- Many guests have suffered from strange and unusual deaths while staying at the motel.

- The ghost of an overdose victim continues to haunt the place where her life ended.

History

1965 – Claude Howard opened Howard's Townhouse Restaurant.

1968 – A brawl took place in the parking lot of Howard's Townhouse in which a group of men beat Lamont Haack to death.

1971 – Claude Howard sold the restaurant to John Ceritto. Mr. Ceritto renamed the business "Mr. C's."

1970s – John Ceritto sold the business to its current owner, Fedil "Fred" Elezi. The restaurant's name was again changed as Mr. Elezi renamed it The Red Apple.

1978 to 1980 – King's Towing was located in the parking lot. King's Towing also served as Wayne's impound lot.

1987 to 1990 – The Red Apple Inn motel was constructed on the site of the towing company.

1997 – A woman died from a heroin overdose in the Red Apple Inn.

2000s – A female guest died in room 221 while having sex with her husband.

2000s – A hotel guest chocked to death on the pizza he was eating.

2008 – A hotel guest overdosed on drugs while staying at the inn.

Today – The motel is open to the public.

Source: Wayne Historical Museum

Investigation

The owner of the Red Apple told us that for years he has heard the legend of room 117 being haunted. He is uncertain as to the origin of the legend, but several times a year ghost research groups spend the night in the room in hopes of capturing evidence of the playful ghost. It appears that the room is haunted by a mischievous spirit who likes to hide items, move guests' personal belongings, and create knockings and other odd noises inside the room.

One popular legend of room 117 that has been circulating for years is the story of the death of a man named Charles "Chick" McGee. Legends state that Chick was a guest at the Red Apple and decided to walk over to grab a bite to eat at the Red Apple Restaurant. Later that evening, Chick was found stabbed to death inside room 117. The case was never solved, but it was rumored that Chick was killed by an angry waitress who was stiffed on her tip. Chick's ghost now is said to hide the TV remote and is blamed for shampoo, soap, and other items being moved and hidden throughout the room. Other guests of the inn have reported hearing unusual knockings on the walls and other mysterious noises coming from inside their rooms.

As far fetched as the story sounds, it has been posted on numerous ghost research sites. We found no evidence of anyone being murdered inside the hotel. It is also an odd coincidence that the name Charles "Chick" McGee is the name of a permanent character on the widely popular national radio program known for its hijinks called *The Bob & Tom Show.*

Perhaps the story has been changed or mistaken from the real murder that occurred in the parking lot of where the Red Apple Inn now sits. According to the *Wayne Eagle Newspaper* on July 21st, 1968, Lamont Haack was pulling out of his parking space when a man threw a punch at him. Haack, a large man, jumped out of his car to confront the man and was attacked by a group of seven to nine other men. While he was on the ground he was repeatedly kicked and punched. Two men came to his aid but they were beaten back by the group. Later that night, Haack died from his injuries. Witnesses reported that the assailants escaped in a Red Ford Torino and a 1964 Cadillac Convertible. The case remains unsolved.

Lamont Haack was not the only one to die on the property, as the inn has been home to several strange deaths over the years. A few years back, a married couple had booked room 221 for the night. Later in the evening an ambulance was called to the room. When the paramedics got there they found out that the woman had died while having sex with her husband. The Wayne Historical Museum also told the story of a woman who died from a heroine overdose while staying at the hotel in 1997. In 2008, two more guests died during their stay at the inn. One unlucky man was found dead in his room after he chocked to death on the pizza he was eating, while yet another guest was found dead in his room from a drug overdose.

SOUTHWEST
MICHIGAN

Grill House Restaurant

Location: Allegan, Allegan County, Michigan
Address: 1071 32nd St., Allegan, MI 49010-9157
Phone: (269) 686-9192
Website: www.grillhouse.net
Facebook: www.facebook.com/pages/The-Grill-House/113518752015764

Ghost Lore

A lot of people "don't know Jack." But that's not the case at the Grill House in Allegan. It's believed the bar and restaurant are haunted by a whiskey-drinking lumberjack affectionately known to the regulars as "Jack."

- In empty rooms, chairs will slide across the floor.

- Doors mysteriously open and close.

- Patrons have felt their legs touched and feet pulled by invisible hands.

- Lights, TVs, radios, and faucets will turn on and off by themselves.

- Stations on the radio change on their own.

- Dishes will rattle when nobody is around.

- Knocks are heard on the walls.

- Bar glasses will fly across the room.

History

1833 – Allegan's first settler, Elisha Ely, arrived.

1834 – Samuel Hubbard purchased thousands of acres in the area.

1836 – The Hubbard House was built.

1838 – Hubbard's company developed the village of Allegan.

1847 – Hubbard died in Boston at the age of 62.

1847 – According to legend, a lumberjack was killed in a barroom knife fight at the Hubbard House.

1973 – Dr. William K. Wellman purchased the property and restored the building. It opened as the Hubbard House Restaurant.

1996 – Margo McHattie purchased the building and the 21 acres it sits on. She put a gourmet restaurant in the basement and an art gallery on the main floor. The business was renamed the Painted Lady.

1998 – The current owners, Dan and Marcia Wagner, purchased the property and named it the Grill House.

2008 – The Grill House was featured on the Travel Channel's *Food Paradise* program (see episode "Steak Paradise: A Second Helping," air date: December 10, 2008).

2012 – The Destination America channel's program *United States of Food*, hosted by chef Todd Fisher, also did a feature on the Grill House (see episode "United States of Steaks," air date: July 22, 2012).

Investigation

The Hubbard House.   Samuel Hubbard was born in Boston in 1785. He was married twice, and between the two wives he had fathered 11 children. He served as a Massachusetts Supreme Court Judge from 1842-47 and dabbled in real estate and land speculation.

In 1833, Allegan's first settler, Elisha Ely, arrived to prospect the area. He sent word to his Eastern backers about the area's potential for lumbering. One of those backers was Hubbard. The following year, Hubbard and the other backers purchased thousands of acres in the region. In 1836, the Hubbard House was built. It was originally used as a headquarters for Hubbard's company, but it also served as a stagecoach stop and boarding house for the lumberjacks who came to the area to work. In 1838, Hubbard's company developed the village of Allegan. The name was made up by Henry Rowe Schoolcraft who wanted something that sounded like a Native American word. In 1847, Hubbard died in Boston at the age of 62.

Over the years, the Hubbard House served as a sawmill, tenement house, and farmhouse. In 1973, Dr. William K. Wellman purchased the property primarily for the land, then decided to restore the building and open it as the Hubbard House Restaurant. Wellman was well-known to the community as a veterinarian, racing stable owner, writer, artist, and craftsman. In the summer of 1996, Margo McHattie, a single mother of two, purchased the building and opened it as a restaurant and art gallery called the Painted Lady. During renovation, she planned to build an elevator for disabled customers, but before excavation began, she was careful to make an offering of tobacco to Mother Earth. She had heard about the building's reputation for ghostly activities and didn't want to take any chances. The current owners, Dan and Marcia Wagner, purchased the property in 1998 and renamed it the Grill House. The basement contains the Rock Bottom bar, and the main floor is a unique steakhouse where the customer selects and grills their own steak.

The Legend of Jack. "Jack" is the nickname given to the legendary ghost of a lumberjack who was killed in a barroom knife fight in 1847 at the Hubbard House. Supposedly his body was buried in an unmarked grave on the property. Although we've been unable to find documentation to confirm the legend, the haunting activity is frequent and undeniable. Over the years, full-bodied apparitions of Jack have been seen by owners, employees, and patrons, and witnesses have always been consistent in their descriptions. He appears as a six-foot-tall man with dark hair, wearing dark pants and a white shirt. Sometimes the staff will arrive early in the morning and find a single shot of whiskey, Jack's drink of choice, sitting on the bar. It's his signature trademark to let people know he's still around.

The Old Regent Theatre

Location: Allegan, Allegan County, Michigan
Address: 211 Trowbridge Street, Allegan, MI 49010-1306
Phone: (269) 673-2737
Facebook: www.facebook.com/OldRegentTheatre

Ghost Lore

In theatres today, 3-D movies are all the craze, but at the Old Regent Theatre, you might experience something from beyond the third dimension. Moviegoers have been known to encounter things that seem to jump out not only from the screen, but from another realm.

- Patrons have seen full-bodied apparitions—sometimes sitting in the seat next to them—that vanish before their eyes.

111

- Cold spots have been felt in various parts of the theatre.
- People have had the feeling of not being alone.
- A shadow person has been seen in the projection room.
- People have felt the physical touch of a cold, invisible hand.
- Witnesses have seen moving forms.
- Afterhours, employees have heard the sound of laughter in the empty building.

History

1888 – The building was originally constructed as a horse livery stable.

1902 – It was converted into a Buick garage.

1919 – It became a vaudeville theatre and also showed silent films.

1930s – It was renovated in the art deco style made famous by the 1925 Paris World's Fair and reopened as primarily a movie theatre.

1980s – Due to mismanagement, the theatre closed and sat empty for several years.

1990 – It was scheduled for demolition but received a last minute reprieve when a nonprofit organization, The Old Regent Theatre Company, purchased it and restored it to the grandeur of its 1930's appearance.

1996 – The theatre reopened.

1997 – A storm resulted in the collapse of the roof—just one hour after the theatre had closed for the night. The city of Allegan paid off the remaining mortgage of $18,000, and, through grants, the theatre was repaired and restored.

1999 – The theatre reopened.

2007 – The original marquee was restored.

Today – The theatre is in business and shows classic and first-run films, and has a children's matinee on Saturday and Sunday afternoons. They still use the movie screen that measures 20 feet by 30 feet and is now one of the largest screens remaining in Michigan.

Investigation

During its long history, the building has served as a livery, garage, and theatre, so it's difficult to determine the historical source of the haunting activity. Regardless, it seems the hauntings were activated by the 1990 restoration project. Ghosts have been seen, heard, and felt by patrons and employees of the theatre. Occasionally, people will see the apparition of a young woman who vanishes before their eyes, but the most common manifestation is the feeling of being touched when no one is around. Ghost investigators have captured EVPs (electronic voice phenomenon) and documented the cold spots with thermal scanners.

Beckwith Theatre

Location: Dowagiac, Cass County, Michigan
Address: 100 New York Ave., Dowagiac, MI 49047-1756
Phone: (269) 782-ROLE (7653)
Email: info@beckwiththeatre.com
Website: www.beckwiththeatre.com
Facebook: www.facebook.com/BTC100

Ghost Lore

At one time, this old building was a Methodist Church, but now the altar area has been converted into a stage for performers. The many haunting experiences here have caused the Beckwith Theatre Company to wonder if maybe ghostly choirs from the past are there to audition for musicals.

- When alone in the theatre, people have heard their name called out.

- People have heard the sound of ghosts singing. Sometimes it's popular musicals, other times it's old hymns.

- Apparitions have been seen.

- Prankish activity has occurred. Belongings and props have been moved and sometimes hidden. Ghosts playfully hide objects such as car keys and scissors.

- The piano has played on its own.

- When people step into the kitchen, the light has sometimes turned on by itself.

- A ghost of a young orphan girl has been seen in the stairwell. Research states that when alive, she had arrived from New York on the Orphan Train during the Great Depression.

- People have heard the sound of the girl whispering or laughing.

- Handwriting has appeared on scripts and notebooks left in the building overnight.

- During a séance with a Ouija Board, the performers witnessed a shadow person.

History

1871 – The Round Oak Stove Company was founded in Dowagiac by Philo D. Beckwith. It manufactured what was considered the finest heating stove money could buy. The company was very successful, and at its height employed 1200 of the 5000 residents in Dowagiac. The company continued to produce stoves until 1946.

1889 – Beckwith died at the age of 54.

1892 – In memory of the late Beckwith, his family built the Beckwith Memorial Theatre in downtown Dowagiac at Front and Beeson streets. In its heyday, it attracted an impressive array of national talent. Lillian Russell sang arias on its stage, and in 1911, John Philip Sousa directed a performance of the "1812 Overture." In 1966, the Beckwith Memorial Theatre was demolished. A parking lot now occupies the site.

1925 – The First United Methodist Church building was constructed. From 1925 to 1929, the Orphan Train brought orphans from New York to the church. Later the building became a Knights of Columbus hall.

1990 – A community theatre company was formed and acquired the building for $30,000. It adopted the Beckwith name.

Investigation

Most often encountered is the spirit of a young girl believed to have been dropped off at the building when the Orphan Train arrived in town. The Orphan Train Movement, a U.S. program ran from 1853 to 1929, transported orphaned and vagrant children from larger cities, like New York, to foster homes in small towns around the country. It's estimated that a quarter of a million children were relocated through this program.

The theatre consists of the main floor and a basement. On more than one occasion, theatre workers were going down the steps when they encountered a young girl huddled at the bottom of the stairs. The girl looks terrified as she crouchs on the floor with a blanket wrapped around her. She appears to be in her early teens and usually has a sullen expression on her face.

Felt Mansion

Location: Holland, Allegan County, Michigan
Physical Address: 6597 138th Ave., Holland, MI 49423
Mailing Address: Laketown Township Office, 4338 Beeline Rd., Holland, MI 49423-9719
Phone: (616) 335-8982 for tours; (616) 335-3050 for rentals
Email: events@feltmansion.org
Website: www.feltmansion.org
Facebook: www.facebook.com/pages/The-Felt-Estate-and-Shore-Acres-Farm/75736212293

Ghost Lore

Dorr Felt was the nerdy Bill Gates or Steve Jobs of his time. Like them, he was an entrepreneur who dropped out of school and went on to make a fortune by developing a new technology. The Felt Mansion, with its 25 rooms and third-story ballroom, was merely the summer home for the Chicago family. Mr. Felt built it for his beloved wife Agnes, who, sadly, died a few weeks later and never

117

really had a chance to enjoy the mansion. However, many believe she has returned, at least in spirit, to spend eternity in her beautiful home.

- Shadow people have been seen dancing in the ballroom.

- Full-blown apparitions of Agnes Felt appear throughout the mansion.

- Sounds of voices and moaning have been heard.

- The door to Agnes' room will sometimes open and slam shut on its own.

- Faces have been seen looking out of the upstairs windows.

- Footsteps have been heard in empty hallways.

- Orbs and mists appear in photos.

- Ghosts have been seen outdoors near the fountain.

The third-floor ballroom.

History

1862 – Dorr Eugene Felt was born in Newark, Wisconsin.

1863 – Agnes McNulty was born in Bellevue, Iowa.

1876 – At the age of 14, Dorr Felt dropped out of high school.

1880 – At age 18, he moved to Chicago with 50 cents in his pocket.

1884 – At age 22, he became a self-made millionaire when he invented the Comptometer (the world's first multiple-column, key-operated machine) and the Comptograph (the first practical adding/listing machine).

1891 – Dorr and Agnes got married in Chicago. They went on to have four daughters: Virginia (1892), Elizabeth (1893), Constance (1896), and Dorothea (1903).

1919 – He purchased several hundred acres on Lake Michigan between Holland and Saugatuck.

1925 – He began construction on the summer home for his wife Agnes.

1928 – The construction of the 17,000 square foot mansion was completed, and they moved in. It had 25 rooms and a third-floor ballroom. Six weeks later, Agnes died of a stroke at the age of 67.

1929 – Dorr married a French woman, Jeanne Marie Jean Josephine Saurin Watkins, in Paris.

1930 – At the age of 68, Dorr died of a heart attack in Chicago.

1949 – The family sold the business. The mansion was sold to the St. Augustine Seminary for boys.

1960s – After a school was built nearby, the nuns who worked at the school lived in the mansion.

1970s – The State of Michigan used the property for a State Police post. They tore down the boy's school and replaced it with the Dunes Correctional Facility.

1996 – The township bought the house from the state for $1.

2001 – The West Michigan Ghost Hunters Society gave public ghost tours to raise money for the restoration of the house. They generated over $3,000.

2002 – Pat Hoezee Meyer and her husband Dean started a restoration campaign for the mansion.

Today – The house is open for public tours and can be rented for weddings and other large events. The restoration is ongoing.

Investigation

Most of the haunting activity began after renovation of the mansion had started. In 2001, the West Michigan Ghost Hunters Society conducted public ghost tours of the estate to raise money for the completion of the restoration. Late one Halloween night, they teamed up with the SouthEast Michigan Ghost Hunters Society to do an investigation in the ballroom. At one point, the group witnessed a shadow person that appeared out of nowhere and was making a sweeping motion, as if holding a broom. A moment later, a second shadow person appeared next to it. The investigators watched the pair for several minutes until both vanished before their eyes. During another investigation, the team placed a video camera on a chair facing into Agnes' room and captured on tape a heavy French door closing and opening on its own. The video became known as the "Merle Incident" and can be viewed on YouTube at www.youtube.com/watch?v=YbhfYxgE6ik.

McCourtie Park

Location: Somerset Center, Hillsdale County, Michigan
AKA: Aiden Lair, W.H.L. McCourtie Estate, Laiden
Physical Address: 10436 South Jackson Road, Somerset Center, MI 49282
Phone: (517) 688-9223
Facebook:
www.facebook.com/pages/McCourtie-Park/100575140029949
Directions: From Hwy. 12 (Chicago Rd.), turn north on S. Jackson Rd. Drive .3 miles. The park will be on the left.

Ghost Lore

Bridges represent transitions. "Crossing over" is a euphemism for taking that journey from life to death. Bridges are also commonly associated with hauntings, and in our investigations we've come across numerous haunted bridges. But this is the first haunted location we've found that has 17 bridges.

- Camera batteries have failed.

- Disembodied voices have been heard.

- A woman wearing a blue dress and black bonnet has been seen walking through the park.

- There are rumors that a child drowned in one of the ponds. One witness saw a little girl alone in the park. When approached, the girl ran away and disappeared into the woods.

History

1872 – William Herbert Lee (W.H.L.) McCourtie was born in Somerset Center.

1886 – He married Ellen Daisy Hulett.

1897 – He was introduced to the cement industry by W.F. Cowhan of Jackson. He moved to Dallas, Texas, where he made a fortune speculating in oil and established the Trinity Portland Cement Company.

1903 – After moving back to Michigan, W.H.L. and Ellen had a son, Wendall Herbert Lee McCourtie.

1920s – The family moved back to Somerset Center.

1924 – McCourtie acquired his family's home and turned the 42-acre estate (once called Laiden or Aiden Lair) into a community showplace.

1930 – McCourtie hired Mexican-American artisans to construct 17 bridges on his property. A rathskeller (underground tavern) and birdhouses were also added.

1933 – McCourtie died in Battle Creek at the age of 61 and was buried in the Somerset Center Cemetery.

1943 – Their son died at the age of 41.

1956 – Ellen died at the age of 82 and was buried in the mausoleum with her husband. After her death, ownership of the park changed hands several times and eventually fell into disrepair.

1987 – The Somerset Township Recreational Authority acquired the estate and restored it.

1992 – It was listed with the National Register of Historic Places.

Today – The park is open to the public.

Investigation

W.H.L. McCourtie was a self-made millionaire and humanitarian. While in Texas, he started a cement company, and after making a fortune, he returned to his hometown of Somerset Center and turned his family estate into a community showplace. At the height of the Great Depression, he provided the town with free entertainment consisting of stunt flyers, baseball, local musicians, dancing, and unlimited refreshments. He billed it as a place "Where Friends Meet Friends and Part More Friendly."

During his renovation of the estate, he hired three Mexican-American folk sculptors to create 17 folk art cement pedestrian

The *el trabejo rustico* chimneys disguised as trees.

bridges over a creek and wetlands on his property. In building the bridges, they also created what is most likely the largest U.S. collection of *el trabejo rustico*, which is the Mexican folk tradition of sculpting concrete to look like wood.

McCourtie also built a rathskeller, which is an underground tavern or restaurant where beer was served. During the Prohibition, Highway 12, which ran through Somerset Center, was an important link between Chicago and Detroit, and the rathskeller functioned as a speakeasy. McCourtie held several parties that included smoking, drinking, and poker playing with bigwigs from Detroit, such as Henry Ford. According to legend, Al Capone and other high-ranking criminals from Chicago were also guests. Because the building was built underground and faced away from the street, the police were unable to see it. Two concrete trees, made to look like dead trees, were built on top and blended in with the background. The trees were hollow and doubled as chimneys for the stills. In the back of the underground hideout are tunnels once used for bootlegging.

The rathskeller where people have seen the ghostly "Lady in Blue" enter through the middle door.

The Lady in Blue. The most famous ghost in the park is an apparition known as the "Lady in Blue," "Lady in Black," or "Lady in the Shed." Occasionally, she's seen walking across the concrete bridges, but most often she's been seen entering or exiting the rathskeller through the middle door, usually in broad daylight. She's described as petite and wearing old-fashioned clothing that consists of a black bonnet and a long dress that's sometimes seen as blue but other times as black. Suspecting the ghost could be Ellen, the wife of W.H.L. McCourtie, we conducted an extensive search for a photo of her. When we finally found one, we were surprised to see she was wearing a huge bonnet, which matches the descriptions of the apparition.

Ellen McCourtie (1873-1956)

UPPER
PENINSULA
MICHIGAN

Big Bay Point Lighthouse

Location: Big Bay, Marquette County, Michigan
Address: Big Bay Point Lighthouse Bed & Breakfast,
3 Lighthouse Road, Big Bay, MI 49808
Phone: (906) 345-9957
Fax: (906) 345-9418
Email: keepers@BigBayLighthouse.com
Website: www.bigbaylighthouse.com
Innkeepers: Jeff and Linda Gamble

Directions: Drive 28 miles north of Marquette. The inn is off CR 550, at the end of the road.

Ghost Lore

One of the guests at the Big Bay Lighthouse Bed and Breakfast has been there since 1896, and the owners have no intentions of evicting him. Not only is this the only bed and breakfast that's an active lighthouse, it's also haunted. It was named one of the "Top

10 Haunted Lighthouses" by *Coastal Living* magazine.   This secluded retreat offers seven rooms, a living room with fireplace, library, sauna, hiking trails, and, did I mention, ghosts.   If you're looking for romance and thrills, this place will definitely provide the thrills.

- Water faucets and showers will turn on and off by themselves.

- Doors will open and slam.

- Banging sounds come from inside the building.

- A red-haired man has been seen in the lighthouse.

- People have heard strange scraping sounds in the building.

- A man dressed in a lighthouse keeper's uniform has been seen walking in the yard.

- Guests have heard the sound of footsteps when nobody is present.

- The ghost likes to slam kitchen cabinet doors.

- Strange noises have been heard outside.

- Guests have seen a red-haired man reflected in the mirror.

History

1896 – Construction of the Big Bay Point Lighthouse and the keeper's house was completed at a cost of $25,000. William Prior was the first lighthouse keeper.

1901 – Prior's son George worked as his assistant but died after sustaining an injury. Prior abandoned the lighthouse and disappeared in the woods.

1902 – A hunter found Prior's remains in the woods.

1944 – The lighthouse was automated and no longer manned. The light was moved from the tower to a steel post in the northeast corner of the front yard.

1951 – The buildings and land were leased to the US Army for two years. Soldiers camped-out in the meadow and woods to the west of the lighthouse.

1952 – A soldier stationed at the lighthouse committed a murder at the Lumberjack Tavern in Big Bay.

1961 – The lighthouse and keeper's house sat vacant for six years and fell into disrepair. The property was purchased by a Dr. John Pick (via sealed bid) for $40,000. Dr. Pick was a plastic surgeon from Chicago who promoted his professional services with the line, "You can't choose your face, but you can 'Pick' your nose." During his seventeen year restoration of the building, he installed indoor plumbing, electricity, and a modern heating system.

1979 – The doctor, who was in his 80s and in poor health, sold it to Dan Hitchens of Traverse City. Hitchens began renovations to convert it into a bed and breakfast. He added bathrooms to most of the seven bedrooms and a sauna in the tower.

1984 – Hitchens sold the lighthouse to an investment group of whom the managing owners were Norman "Buck" Gotschall, and his wife. They completed the work of converting it into a bed and breakfast.

1986 – The Big Bay Point Lighthouse Bed and Breakfast officially opened.

1991 – Nearing retirement, the Gotschalls and their partners sold the lighthouse to the fourth and present owners, John Gale, Linda Gamble, and Jeff Gamble.

2011 – Big Bay Lighthouse was placed on the market for $1,275,000.

Investigation

There have been at least two notable deaths associated with the lighthouse. Both have given rise to the belief that the lighthouse is haunted.

William Prior. In 1880, George and Ester Prior immigrated from Hampshire, England to Marquette, Michigan with their three sons and two daughters. All three boys went on to become lighthouse keepers on Lake Superior. The oldest son, red-haired William Henry Prior, was the head keeper at Stannard's Rock Lighthouse, but on August 15, 1896 he was transferred to Big Bay Lighthouse. Unable to find a reliable assistant, he finally appointed his 19-year-old son, George Edward Prior, as 1st Assistant Keeper in 1900. In April of 1901, young George fell down the stairs and seriously injured his leg. William didn't immediately bring his son to the hospital because he was unwilling to abandon his responsibility of maintaining the light. The lighthouse was only accessible by water, and there was no means of outside communication. This left them for the most part completely isolated until somebody arrived to bring supplies. It was two months before Prior brought his son to the Marquette Hospital. By that time the wound was heavily infected and gangrene had set in. A few days later, on June 14, George died.

After the funeral, William returned to his job at the lighthouse but immediately disappeared into the woods with a gun and a bottle of strychnine. Seventeen months later, on September 24, a hunter came upon the decaying remains of his body hanging from a tree about a mile and a half south of the lighthouse; an apparent suicide.

Haunting activity in the lighthouse didn't begin until 1984, after Norman and Marilyn Gotschall purchased the building and converted it into a bed and breakfast. This was when the guests and owners started hearing unexplained noises and seeing a red-haired man dressed in a lighthouse keeper's uniform wandering the property. Current owners, Jeff and Linda Gamble, have also had ghostly encounters with the deceased lighthouse keeper. They say he likes to slam the kitchen cabinet doors in the middle of the night.

Anatomy of a Murder. According to Linda Gamble, the inn is haunted by at least five spirits. One of them may have had a connection to another area death. From 1951 to 1952, the U.S. Army leased the property surrounding the lighthouse. Soldiers were stationed there and trained in anti-aircraft artillery. They installed large guns used for target shooting over the lake. One of those soldiers was 38-year-old Lt. Coleman Alonzo Peterson, a veteran of World War II and the Korean War. While he was away on duty, his wife Charlotte Ann liked to frequent the Lumberjack Tavern in Big Bay. On July 31, 1952, she came home with a bruised body and torn dress and told her husband she was raped by the bartender, Maurice "Mike" Chenoweth, a short, stocky ex-cop, who was known to be a lady's man. Peterson took his German Luger to the tavern, fired six 9 mm bullets into the bartender and calmly walked out. Later that night he was arrested for murder.

Peterson's wife hired former Michigan Supreme Court Justice John D. Voelker to act as her husband's defense attorney. Using the "temporary insanity" plea, Voelker brought in a psychologist, Dr. Thomas Petty, to testify for the defense. Petty argued that due to the shock of hearing his wife had been beaten and raped, Peterson was in a mental state known as "irresistible impulse" and therefore unable to distinguish right from wrong at the time of the shooting. The trial took six days. The jury returned with a verdict of not guilty because of temporary insanity. This was the first time this plea was ever successfully used in Michigan.

Peterson spent only one month in a state asylum for the criminally insane and was freed when they determined he had "regained his sanity." Voelker expected Peterson would be grateful and happy to pay the $3,000 fee to the attorney who so cleverly secured his freedom. However, to his surprise, Peterson had packed up and left town without paying the bill. He left his attorney a note that simply said he had "an irresistible impulse to leave."

Soon afterwards, Peterson divorced his wife, and there were rumors that he had died in a plane crash in Alaska. In fact, he had moved to his father's home state of Texas. While living in San Antonio, he remarried in 1965, then divorced in 1971. In 1977, he died in Corpus Christi at the age of 64.

Using the pen name Robert Traver, Voelker wrote a novel, *Anatomy of a Murder*, which was based on the murder case. It was published in 1958 and remained on the best-seller list for 65 weeks.

In 1959, *Anatomy of a Murder* was released as a film based on the novel. Directed by Otto Preminger, it featured an all-star cast that included James Stewart, Lee Remick, Ben Gazzara, Eve Arden, and George C. Scott. At the time, the film was controversial because of its use of words such as "rape," "contraceptive," and "panties," but it went on to be nominated for seven Academy Awards.

In 1960, a $9 million libel suit was filed against Dell Publishing and Columbia Pictures by Chenoweth's widow and 18-year-old daughter. They alleged the *Anatomy of a Murder* novel and film had caused them to be "held up to public contempt, ridicule, and shame." The following year, a Federal Judge dismissed the case.

Today, tourists can visit the crime scene at the Lumberjack Tavern where some of the movie scenes were shot. Bullet holes can still be seen in the wall, and the police chalk outline where the bartender died remains on the floor . . . although, it's probably been retouched over the years.

Calumet Theatre

Location: Calumet, Houghton County, Michigan
Physical Address: 340 Sixth Street, Calumet, MI 49913
Mailing Address: P.O. Box 167, Calumet, MI 49913-0167
Box Office Phone: (906) 337-2610
Business Office Phone: (906) 337-2166
Fax: (906) 337-3763
Email: boxoffice@calumettheatre.com
Website: www.calumettheatre.com
Facebook:
www.facebook.com/pages/Calumet-Theatre/385143523992

Ghost Lore

Life's but a walking shadow, a poor player
That struts and frets his hour upon the stage
And then is heard no more.

—William Shakespeare, *Macbeth*

Shakespeare compared life to the stage and humans to actors, and implied that after death we are soon forgotten and "heard no more." But in the case of one world-renowned Shakespearean actor, after her death she apparently was heard from again . . . in the very theatre where she once performed *Macbeth*.

- A light in the lobby will shut off on its own.

- Many people have encountered cold spots.

- Workers have heard music in the building when it's empty.

- People have heard the mysterious sound of a loud crash.

The portrait of Helena Modjeska that hangs in the Calumet Theatre. It's said that the haunting activity increases whenever the portrait has been removed.

- A little girl named Elana Rowe died nearby and can be heard screaming.

- In 1903, a man was murdered nearby and can be heard screaming.

- Full-bodied apparitions of actress Helena Modjeska have been seen throughout the theatre.

- Some people immediately sense "a presence" upon entering the theatre.

- The stage curtains will be closed at night, but the staff will sometimes find them wide open in the morning.

History

1875 – The Village of Red Jacket was incorporated.

1898 – The village made plans for an opera house.

1900 – The Red Jacket Village Opera House was constructed and officially opened on March 20. In December, Madam Helena Modjeska performed at the theatre. She would return two more times.

1909 – On April 8, Modjeska died at Newport Beach, California, aged 68, from Bright's disease. She was buried in Poland.

1913 – During the Italian Hall tragedy, the opera house was used as a morgue.

1914 – Vaudeville, legitimate theatre, and silent movies played at the opera house on a regular basis.

1918 – The opera house was closed for two month for cleaning and remodeling during the Spanish Flu epidemic. In November, a fire gutted the stage and destroyed the auditorium chandelier. The opera house was closed for almost four months for repairs.

1929 – The name of the town was changed to Calumet and the opera house became known as the Calumet Theatre. Sound equipment was installed in the theatre and they began showing "talkies" (motion pictures with sound). The theatre provided both movies and stage plays.

1958 – On July 22, Addyse Lane saw the ghost of Madame Modjeska during the opening of *Taming of the Shrew*.

1971 – Motion pictures replaced live theater. The building was designated a Michigan State Historic Site and added to the National Register of Historic Places.

1972 – Summer stock returned.

1975 – The auditorium was restored for Calumet's centennial celebration.

1988 – The exterior of the theatre was restored.

1983 – The Calumet Theatre Company was incorporated as a non-profit organization.

2000 – The theatre celebrated its 100th anniversary.

Investigation

We were unable to verify the stories of the 1903 murder victim or the death of Elana Rowe. Members of the Rowe family have lived in Calumet for many decades, but we were unable to find any documentation for this little girl. Other stories from the theatre are more verifiable.

Italian Hall Disaster. In 1913, The C&H Mining Company was the largest copper mining company in the Upper Peninsula. The Western Federation of Miners established a local union in the area, and by 1913 their membership had grown large enough to effectively strike. Five months into the strike, on December 24, the miners and their families held a Christmas Eve party on the second floor of Calumet's Italian Hall. In the room packed with over 400 people, someone falsely shouted "fire!" creating panic and a human stampede in which seventy-three men, women, and children were crushed to death. Fifty-nine of the victims were children. It's believed that the man who yelled "fire" was an anti-union ally of mine management whose intent was to disrupt the party. Because

The center light in the lobby will turn off and on by itself.
Changing the light bulb and rewiring the fixture has not
made a difference.

the high body count was more than the Calumet funeral home could handle, it was necessary to use the Calumet Theatre as a temporary morgue. Bodies were laid out in the adjoining theatre's main auditorium. Some believe the theatre's haunting activity is directly related to this event.

The Ghost of Helena Modjeska. The renowned actress Helena Modjeska (1840-1909) was born in Poland. She made her stage debut at age 21 and went on to become the reigning diva of Polish national theater, specializing in Shakespearean and tragic roles. In 1876, she emigrated to the U.S. Despite her strong accent and limited English, she achieved great success in this country as well. Throughout the 1880s and 90s, she was the most prominent female Shakespearian actor on the American stage. On December 6, 1900, she performed *Mary Stuart* and *Macbeth* at the Calumet Theatre. In the years following, she returned to the Calumet stage two more times. She died in 1909 at Newport Beach, California, at age 68, from Bright's disease, and her remains were shipped to Poland for burial in the family plot.

On July 22, 1958, the actress Addyse Lane saw the ghost of Madame Modjeska at the Calumet Theatre. Lane was playing the lead role in a summer production of the *Taming of the Shrew*. Near the end of the play she forgot her lines and froze with fear. Gazing up towards the balcony, she saw an apparition of Modjeska, who gave her her lines. It had always been Modjeska's ambition to one day do *Taming of the Shrew*, but she never had the chance. Apparently helping Lane was her way of finally being a part of the performance.

House of Ludington

Location: Escanaba, Delta County, Michigan
Address: 223 Ludington Street, Escanaba, MI 49829-4027
Phone: (906) 786-6300
Email: HofL@dsnet.us
Website: www.houseofludington.com

Ghost Lore

Many in Escanaba still talk about chef Pat Hayes, the former owner of the House of Ludington. Hayes was the Gordon Ramsey of his day. In fact, Ramsey is a pussy cat in comparison. People described Hayes as off-the-wall and spirited, but now some believe he is a spirit who watches over his beloved establishment and occasionally likes to prank his guests.

- Patrons have heard the sound of footsteps when nobody is there.

- The glass elevator has been known to travel up and down on its own.

- People have seen apparitions of Pat Hayes.

- Doorknobs mysteriously rattle, and doors shake.

- Guests have encountered cold spots that sometimes follow them.

- Lights, TVs, and faucets turn on and off by themselves.

- Toilets flush on their own.

- Hotel guests have had the bed covers pulled off their bed by unseen hands.

- People have heard strange sounds and voices in rooms that are empty.

History

1864 – Irish immigrant E. Gaynor built the Gaynor House Hotel.

1871 – He renamed it the Ludington House, after lumberman Nelson Ludington (1818 to 1883) who owned the largest sawmill in Escanaba.

1879 – Gaynor sold the hotel, and for six years there was a succession of different owners.

1885 – It was purchased by John Christie.

1887 – Christie rebuilt the hotel as a brick structure in the Queen Anne style and added a wing on the west side. It was expanded to 100 rooms. He renamed it the New Ludington Hotel. It now featured baths, steam heat, electric call bells, and gas lights—all for $2 a day.

1939 – Harold Clement "Pat" Hayes, an Irishman from Chicago, bought the hotel. When Hayes bought the hotel, it was boarded up, rundown, and bankrupt. A short year later, Duncan Hines recommended the Ludington as the best place to eat in Michigan, and Hayes became known as "Michigan's Most Famous Chef."

1948 – The hotel name was changed to House of Ludington.

1959 – Hayes installed the external glass-walled elevator.

1969 – Hayes died of cancer on January 27. His will left the hotel to Bea Gallagher and Mary Dowling, two women who ran the business. A decade later, they filed for bankruptcy and lost the hotel.

1982 – It was purchased at auction by Gerald and Vernice Lancour who extensively remodeled and redecorated it. Gerald's son, Cary Brian Lancour, managed the hotel.

1996 – In February, the hotel was closed and sat vacant.

1998 – After Lancour was sentenced to one year in jail for filing a false tax return and for unemployment fraud, the hotel was purchased and reopened by Edward and Suzell Eisenberger who continue to run the hotel today.

Investigation

The hotel has an impressive list of past guests: Henry Ford, Johnny Cash, John Sousa, Patricia Neal, Prince Bertil of Sweden, Jimmy Hoffa, Guy Lombardo, Randy Travis, George Gobel, Lynn Dickey, and many others. It has also been owned by a number of colorful characters. When John Christie was the hotel's proprietor back in the 1880s, a circus came into town, and Christie kept an elephant as collateral on an unpaid bill.

Pat Hayes. Without a doubt, the most memorable of the previous owners was Harold Clement Hayes, known to most people as "Pat." Born in South Boston, Massachusetts, he was of Irish ancestry. Later, he moved to Canada and was a student at the University of Toronto when he quit school to join Canada's Royal Flying Corps during WWI, spending a year in France as a squadron leader. While in France, he received 16 stitches when his chin was grazed by a bullet. After the war, he moved to Chicago and was employed with the Albert Pick Company and sold kitchen equipment to hotels. It was his job to travel around and show chefs how to cook with the equipment. During the Great Depression, Albert Pick got into the hotel business and the Pick chain grew.

This gave Hayes his first taste of the hotel business, and he eventually went on to own the Pershing Hotel in Chicago and the Hotel Julian in Dubuque, Iowa. In 1939, he moved to Escanaba to run the Gambrinus Brewery, but instead chose to sell the beer factory and buy the Ludington Hotel.

It was not uncommon for him to throw customers out of his restaurant for ordering their steak on the burned side, shouting "that's no way to treat fine meat!" One prominent woman refused to return to his restaurant after she sent her too rare steak back to the kitchen, and Hayes humiliated her by sending back a plate of chicken.

Behind the bar, he posted a sign that read: "Gentlemen, to your health! Your drinks are limited" and limited customers to two Manhattans or two good-sized martinis. One of his bartenders explained, "We run a cocktail lounge, not an embalming parlor." Hayes argued that a drunk could never appreciate the taste of such delicacies as squab baked in cantaloupe.

He entertained several famous guests at the hotel and restaurant. When one of them, Prince Bertil of Sweden, ordered a rare wine that Hayes did not stock, Hayes immediately had a bottle flown up from Chicago just in time for dinner.

For a short time, Hayes was involved in politics. He advocated making the Upper Peninsula a new state named "Superior." Later, perhaps tongue-in-cheek, he suggested the U.P. secede from the U.S. and become a separate nation in order to qualify for foreign aid.

Another time he proposed a harness race between a horse and a deer. He even went as far as training a deer to pull a sulky, until the State Conservation Department put an end to his endeavor.

Hayes had known ties to Al Capone. Before moving to Escanaba, Hayes once ran the Metropole Hotel in Chicago where Capone stayed, and was apparently Capone's personal chef. Over the years, a number of rumors circulated:

- Al Capone used to frequent the Ludington Hotel whenever he made trips to the Upper Peninsula.

- Capone had someone killed at the hotel.

- Somewhere in the hotel, bullet holes are still in the wall.

- Bootleg whiskey was smuggled into the hotel through underground tunnels that led out to a dock on Lake Michigan.

- The tunnels also served as an escape route for Capone, in the event of a police raid.

- A secret cache of booze is still hidden somewhere behind the hotel walls.

During his lifetime, Hayes would neither deny nor confirm the rumors. We do know from his bookkeepers that Hayes operated the hotel in the red, managing to keep it open with money from "outside" and "unidentified" sources.

The Hauntings. The hotel's glass elevator was Pat Hayes' pride and joy. He had it installed in 1959, and it was the first of its kind in Michigan. The owners told us it was common for the elevator to activate on its own and go from floor to floor. Usually it stops at the second floor. The doors open and close, as if some invisible entity is either getting on or off. Workmen have carefully inspected the elevator numerous times, but have never found a malfunction or explanation for this curious phenomenon.

In the book, *A Ghostly Road Tour*, Escanaba resident Jan Langley describes some of the haunting experiences of the Ludington employees. When a young woman was working part-time at the restaurant, she was walking down a hallway when she felt as if she was grabbed by cold, invisible hands. At that moment, she noticed a large oil painting of chef Pat Hayes on the wall and wondered how it was possible that she had never noticed it before. When she mentioned it to her co-workers, nobody knew what she was talking about. They went to look at the painting only to find an empty wall. Years later, while rummaging through piles of furniture stored on the third floor, somebody found the painting described by the worker. Today, it's displayed on the wall where she originally saw it.

On another occasion, a waitress couldn't find daycare and had to bring her four-year-old daughter to work with her. She put the girl in a highchair while she waited on tables. Later, she noticed her daughter eating green olives—the child's favorite snack—and inquired as to who gave them to her. The girl answered, explaining that "the white ghost-man did." After work, the mother was carrying her daughter down the hallway when the little girl pointed to the oil painting of Pat Hayes and identified him as "the nice ghost-man."

The Dare. If you spend the night in one of the rooms, hang a wind chill in the doorway. It will alert you when the spirit of Pat Hayes is present.

Grand Hotel

Location: Mackinac Island, Mackinac County, Michigan
Address: 286 Grand Avenue, Mackinac Island, MI 49757
Phone: (906) 847-3331
Toll-Free: 1-800-33-GRAND or 1-800-334-7263
Fax: (906) 847-3259
Email: email@grandhotel.com
Website: www.grandhotel.com
Facebook: www.facebook.com/grandhotel

Ghost Lore

One thing we learned from the 1982 film *Poltergeist* is that you shouldn't build on top of a cemetery. If you do, make sure you move all the bodies first; otherwise, you could expect some haunting activity. The luxurious Grand Hotel was built specifically to cater to the wealthier tourists that came to the island to relax in peace. Sometimes that peace gets interrupted.

- Doors will shake and sometimes open and close on their own.
- People have heard phantom footsteps in empty hallways and other strange noises.
- Guests have awoken to their beds shaking.
- Electrical appliances, such as lights and blow-dryers, will turn on and off on their own.
- Guests have heard the sound of whispering and sobbing.
- Employees have seen phantom soldiers and other apparitions.
- Guests sometimes get the jitters and sense a presence in their room.
- Apparitions of a woman in black walking her dog have been seen on the porch.
- Guests have found their toiletries and clothes moved to other parts of the room.
- Shadow people and moving shadows have been seen in the rooms.

History

1886 – The Michigan Central Railroad, Grand Rapids and Indiana Railroad, and Detroit and Cleveland Steamship Navigation Company formed the Mackinac Island Hotel Company. They purchased land on Mackinac Island and construction began.

1887 – The hotel opened. Nightly rates ranged from $3-$5 per night. The 660-foot long front porch was the longest in the world.

1890s – The hotel hosted the first public demonstration of Thomas Edison's new invention—the phonograph. Over the years, Edison frequently returned to the hotel to demonstrate other inventions.

1895 – Mark Twain came for a reading in the Hotel's grand salon. Admission was $1.00.

1947 – The film *This Time for Keeps* starring Jimmy Durante and Esther Williams was released. The hotel was the setting for the movie. The hotel pool was later named after Esther Williams.

1980 – The film *Somewhere in Time* starring Christopher Reeve, Jane Seymour, and Christopher Plummer was released. The hotel was used as the backdrop and one of the settings. Every October the hotel hosts an annual convention for the fans of the movie.

2012 – The Grand Hotel celebrated its 125th Anniversary.

Investigation

In the film *Somewhere in Time*, Christopher Reeve's character, Richard Collier, is transported into the past. That is also the feeling most people get during their first visit to the island. Although it wasn't strictly enforced until the 1930s, automobiles have been banned from the entire island since about 1900. The only transportation allowed is bicycles and horse and buggies. This,

coupled with the architecture of the buildings, results in an 18th- and 19th-century atmosphere that seems to draw people into the past and ghosts into the present.

In 1780, when the British took possession of Mackinac Island, it was actually a sacred ancient Indian burial ground known as *Michilimackinac*. When excavation began for the construction of the Grand Hotel, untold numbers of bones were inadvertently dug up. Many of these skeletons were relocated, but it's believed that some still remain under the hotel's foundation.

When the hotel property expanded, one of the original Fort Mackinac Island cemeteries was moved to make room for the horse stables. The bodies were disinterred and most likely moved to the Post Cemetery.

Because the hotel sits on burial grounds, many people believe this to be the cause of the haunting activity by restless spirits. A writer who goes by the name of "The Traveling Assassin," blogged about stories she had heard about the Grand Hotel. She knew who was alone in the hotel theatre when he saw what appeared to be two

19th-century soldiers approaching him. When they were about three feet away, he passed out. When he came to, he found himself laying on the floor with his hands folded across his chest as if in the burial position.

Another time in the theatre, a Hispanic maintenance worker was on the stage when he observed a black, misty form with red eyes hovering over the theatre floor. When it began to move towards him, he perceived that it was evil, and screamed something in Spanish at the entity. When it continued to advance towards him, he fainted and had to spend two days in the Mackinac Island Medical Center.

Todd Clements, author of the popular book *Haunts of Mackinac* and guide for several Mackinac Island ghost tours, knows about several hauntings at the Grand Hotel. He talks about a mysterious woman in black who was a guest at the hotel in 1891. She was accompanied by a large, white Russian wolfhound that she walked up and down the long porch. Nobody knew who she was. On the day that she checked out, a large, black bird perched on the railing outside her room. Since that time, numerous guests and employees have seen apparitions of the woman walking her dog on the front porch . . . then vanishing.

There are stories about an eight-year-old girl named Rebecca falling to her death from a fourth-story window, but to date we've been unable verify the reports. It's said that she haunts the fourth floor and likes to prank people by opening and closing doors.

Holy Family Orphanage

Location: Marquette, Marquette County, Michigan
AKA: Holy Cross Orphanage, Jacques Marquette Building, or Old City Orphanage
Address: Corner of Fisher and Altamont streets, Marquette, MI 49855

Directions: From US-41/M-28, turn onto South 7th Street. Take the first right onto Fisher Street. Drive to the corner of Fischer and Altamont streets.

Ghost Lore

The old brick and sandstone orphanage now sits abandoned and dilapidated, but over the years it housed thousands of children. Stories are whispered alleging abuse and murder that took place within the walls.

Instead of coming in out of the cold like she was told to do, a little girl playing in the snow got lost during a blizzard and had to be rescued. Later she died from pneumonia. It's said that the nuns put her body on display in the lobby to frighten the other children into obedience. The ghost of the girl is sometimes heard sobbing.

Another tragic death that occurred at the orphanage was that of a little boy. The nuns claimed he accidentally drowned, but people became concerned when his lifeless body was kept hidden away in the basement. The suspicion was that he had died from a brutal beating at the hands of one of the sisters. His body was being concealed so no one would see the bruises. It's believed his ghost haunts the basement.

- Phantom children have been seen looking out of the broken windows.

- The sounds of children laughing, playing, and screaming have been heard inside the vacant building.

- Lights have been seen inside the building.

- People have encountered icy cold vapors that float through the building.

- The ghost of a little girl has been seen outside the building.

- Inside the building, people have smelled an odor so repugnant that it induced vomiting.

- The ghost of a young boy has been seen sitting on stairs on the south side of the building.

- Shadow people have been seen inside the building.

- People who have ventured into the basement late at night have reported seeing the boy who drowned. He's described as being surrounded by the glow of an eerie green light. Sometimes he's seen standing; other times he appears to be laying in a casket.

History

1914 – At the cost of $100,000, construction on the Holy Family Orphanage began.

1915 – The orphanage opened and began taking in orphans, 60 of whom were Native American children.

1963 – They took in Cuban refugees.

1967 – Rich Ryan was the last orphan to leave the orphanage. After that, the building continued to be used only as offices.

1982 – The building was abandoned. Phoenix businessman Roger Rinne purchased it with the intentions of converting it into an assisted living facility, but the necessary repairs and renovation were never started. The empty building became an eyesore and a target for vandals.

2008 – The building's condition violated several city blight ordinances and city officials sued Rinne to force him to either repair the building or have it demolished.

2009 – A judge ordered Rinne to pay over $6,000 in cumulative building fines and penalties that he owed the city and called the property a public nuisance and ordered Rinne to repair it. Instead of complying, Rinne filed for bankruptcy.

2011 – Mortgage holders foreclosed on the property at a price of nearly $995,000.

2013 – The Marquette City Commission plans to eventually tear down the orphanage. They applied for a statewide grant to help fund the demolition.

Investigation

We've spoken with some of the former residents of the orphanage and have heard contradictory feelings. Some have fond memories of the time they spent there, but others acknowledged there was some abuse that occurred.

From 1915 to 20, as part of the US government's assimilation program, the Holy Family Orphanage took in Indian children who had been removed from their parents. At the orphanage they were forced to integrate into white culture. Speaking their nature language was forbidden, and they were required to practise Catholicism instead of their native spirituality.

We were unable to find documented evidence of the deaths of the girl with pneumonia or the boy who drowned. Death records can be found for three other orphans. All were accidental, and we found no hint of foul play.

- 1963. Frances Paquette, 11, drowned in the city of Marquette public pool on Saturday, June 29th. She was an orphan from Holy Family Orphanage.

- 1944. Robert Mulrean, 11, died Sunday, June 28th of an injury suffered in a baseball game at the orphanage. His skull was fractured by a baseball bat which slipped from the hands of a playmate.

- 1938. Joseph Koss, 16, drowned at the mouth of the Dead River. More than an hour's resuscitation effort by coast guards failed to bring the boy to life after he fell into the river while playing with a companion. He had left the orphanage just three weeks prior.

During the 50-year history of the orphanage, there may have been other undocumented deaths, especially considering how many children lived there.

The building contains both lead paint and asbestos, which were commonly used at the time of its construction. Lead and asbestos abatement alone would cost hundreds of thousands of dollars. A Marquette engineering firm estimated the total cost to renovate the building would be about $3 million. The cost of demolition would be $1 million. The city plans to tear it down, but for now they're waiting for the necessary funding. Ironically, the building that once housed thousands of orphans now sits abandoned like an orphan.

Warning. You can safely observe the orphanage from the street, but do not trespass or you will be arrested and fined. In addition, the structure is dilapidated and unsafe.

Landmark Inn

Location: Marquette, Marquette County, Michigan
Address: 230 North Front Street, Marquette, MI 49855-4221
Phone: (906) 228-2580 (Reservations)
Toll-free: 1-888-752-6362
Website: www.thelandmarkinn.com
Facebook: www.facebook.com/LandmarkInnMQT

Ghost Lore

Famed aviator Amelia Earhart, first woman to fly solo across the Atlantic Ocean, disappeared July 2, 1937 while attempting to circumnavigate the world. It was one of the greatest unsolved mysteries of the 20th century. There are some, however, who believe they've found the lost pilot . . . in room 502 at the Landmark Inn in Marquette, Michigan.

- People have felt invisible hands tug at their clothing.

- In the lounge, wine glasses have flown across the room and shattered.

- Guests have a sense of being followed when they walk down the hallway late at night.

History

1910 – Plans were made to build what was originally called the Northland Hotel.

1917 – The foundation was started and construction continued for 17 years.

1930 – The hotel opened with over 100 rooms. From the 1930s to the 1960s it was the finest hotel in the Upper Peninsula. It served as the social center of Marquette, and a number of celebrities stayed there, including Duke Ellington, Louis Armstrong, and Peter, Paul, and Mary.

1932 – Amelia Earhart stayed in room 502.

1942 – Abbott and Costello stayed there.

1982 – It fell into disrepair and was closed. It remained boarded up for 13 years.

1995 – Bruce and Christine Pesola purchased the Northland Hotel for $103,000. They began an 18-month major renovation and restoration project at the cost of $6.2 million.

1997 – The Pesolas reopened its doors as the Landmark Inn.

Investigation

The Murder Victim. There are legends of a woman having been murdered near the hotel in 1917. When a husband caught his wife cheating, he killed her and disposed of her body by burying it at the construction site of the soon-to-be-built Northland Hotel. The next morning, workers poured the concrete for the foundation, unwittingly concealing evidence of the crime. People sometimes hear the ghostly sounds of the woman calling out to the construction workers to stop. It's believed her restless spirit

157

wanders the hotel, and she can be heard moaning, screaming, and crying.

The Lilac Room. Most of the haunting activity seems to happen on the sixth floor, which used to be apartments. Years ago, a young librarian was living in the Lilac Room on the sixth floor. She was fast approaching age 30 and concerned about being an old spinster. Then one day, she met the man of her dreams, a handsome sailor, also staying at the inn. The couple quickly fell in love and made plans to get married. Before the wedding, he departed on an ore boat and the entire crew was lost at sea during a violent storm on Lake Superior. It's said that the grieving woman died of a broken heart a few months later. There has been a variety of ghostly activity associated with the Lilac Room and the sixth floor.

- The librarian's ghost has been seen pacing the hallway of the sixth floor. She's described as wearing a long, lilac-colored dress, with her hair pulled back in a bun, and smoking a cigarette.

The Lilac Room

- She's been seen standing at the window, staring at the ore docks, as if waiting for the return of her lover.

- It's believed she doesn't like other men. Often, when a man is staying in the Lilac Room, their room key will not work. When a woman from the front desk goes to the door and uses the same key, it works perfectly.

- Another time a man was staying in the room, he climbed into bed and found metal screws under the sheets. After housekeeping changed the bedding, the screws mysteriously reappeared in his bed.

- The rocking chair in the room has been seen rocking on its own.

- Impressions have been seen in the chair and on the bed as if an invisible person was sitting there.

The Amelia Earhart Room

- The phone in the room will ring in the middle of the night, but nobody will be on the line.

- Other times, the front desk will receive a call from the Lilac Room when the room is vacated. Apparently, the ghost likes to make prank phone calls.

- A married couple spent the night in the room one time, and the husband awoke in the middle of the night to find a woman with her hair in a bun, sitting in the rocking chair, smoking a cigarette.

Amelia Earhart. She was born in 1897 in Kansas and learned to fly before learning to drive because her father thought women were bad drivers. After moving to California at the age of 23, she had her first ride in an airplane, and from that moment, she knew exactly what she wanted to do for the rest of her life. In 1928, she became the first woman to fly across the Atlantic Ocean as a passenger, but that didn't satisfy her. Four years later, she became the first woman to make a *solo* transatlantic flight. After that she was the most famous woman pilot in the world.

That same year, Earhart went on a nation-wide "Flying For Fun" lecture tour. On October 24, 1932, just five months after her history-making flight, she spoke at the Louis G. Kaufman Auditorium in Marquette. While in town, she stayed in Room 502 at the Northland Hotel. Manthei Howe, the women's page editor of the *Mining Journal*, came to her room and interviewed her. Although Earhart had to leave right away the next day, she seemed to be enamored with the city and the U.P., and didn't really want to leave. "I'd like to stay in Marquette a few days," she said. "I'd like to explore this country." True to her word—and back by popular demand—she returned in 1935 to do another lecture. Two years later, she disappeared while attempting to be the first woman to circumnavigate the world, but some believe a part of her still remains in Room 502, now officially known as "The Amelia Earhart Room." Guests who have stayed in the room will sometime awake in the middle of the night to see a full-bodied apparition of Earhart standing at the foot of their bed.

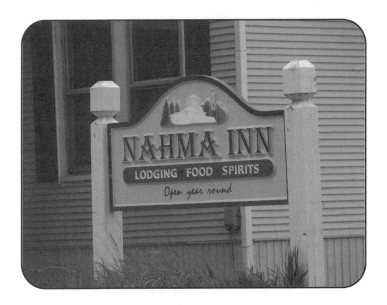

Nahma Inn

Location: Nahma, Delta County, Michigan
Address: 13747 Main Street, Nahma MI 49864
Phone: (906) 644-2486
Fax: (906) 644-2298
Email: NahmaInn@yahoo.com
Website: www.nahmainn.com
Innkeepers: Charley and Laurie MacIntosh
Directions: From west on Hwy 2, turn right on Ee25. Turn right at Gg Rd. Take the first left onto Ll Rd./Main St. Destination will be on right. From east on Hwy 2, turn left on Main St. Drive 1.6 miles to destination on left.

Ghost Lore

The sign for this historic inn advertises "lodging, food, and spirits," and by "spirits," they're not just referring to alcoholic beverages. Many people say the hundred-year-old inn houses the ghost of Miss Nell, a spinster who once taught at the local high school. It's said that the lonely spirit waits patiently, throughout eternity, for a former lover who never returned.

- People have seen the ghost of Miss Nell looking out of the second-story window.

- Guests who stay in her room will leave for a moment and return to find their belongings and the bed to be moved.

- In her room, the ghost will sometimes leave a bodily impression on the bed.

- Footsteps can be heard in the hallway, when nobody is there.

- The ghost will sometimes organize and rearrange things in the kitchen when nobody is around. Other times she's been known to throw things around.

- In the lounge, patrons have witnessed glasses and dishes slide off the tables on their own.

- The ghost is known to walk down the back stairs and out the back door.

- Sometimes her shadow is seen next to her room.

- On rare occasions, the ghost of Charles Good, decked out in a nice suit, is seen walking down the hallway.

History

1881 – The town of Nahma (pronounced NAY-muh) was established by the Bay De Noquet (pronounced Bay de Knock) Lumber Company of Oconto, Wisconsin.

1906 – Originally a boarding house, the inn was built for employees of the lumber company.

1941 – Charles E. Good became the president of the company. He was the fourth generation to own the family business.

1951 – The lumber company shut down, and Good announced the town of Nahma was for sale at a price of $250,000. The town was sold to an Indiana playground manufacturer who had big plans to convert it into a resort. The plans, however, never materialized. The town received national attention when *Life Magazine* did a feature on the sale (see "Sold: One Town," Vol. 31, No. 17, October 22, 1951).

2013 – Nahma once again received national attention when they were featured on the History Channel's *American Pickers* TV program (see "The Doctor Is In," Season 4, Episode 1, Air Date: January 14, 2013). In July of the previous year, the show's hosts, Mike Wolfe and Fred Fritz visited the Nahma Inn and the general store located next door. Both are owned by Charley and Laurie MacIntosh. The pickers were thrilled to rummage through the general store that had been closed for 60 years with its vintage inventory completely intact and with the original cash register.

Investigation

Nahma was built on the shores of Lake Michigan by the Bay de Noquet lumber company for their employees. The name of the town is actually an English corruption of the Ojibwe word for "sturgeon." Charles Ellis Good became the company president in 1941, and he was actually the fourth generation to own the family business. Charles was born in Oconto, Wisconsin in 1887. His parents, Fred and Elizabeth Good, were from Canada. He lived at the Nahma Hotel while running the lumber business, and that's where he met Nellie M. Fleming, another tenant at the hotel. Nellie was born in 1884 in Escanaba, Michigan. She was the daughter of Irish immigrants, Michael and Catherine Fleming. Nellie worked as a teacher at the Nahma high school, and over the years was also employed as a stenographer and clerk. For a while she worked in the hotel kitchen. Nellie and Charles quickly fell in love, and Nellie dreamed they would one day get married, but that never happened.

After 80 years of logging, the available timber supply was exhausted, and by 1951 the lumber company was forced to shut down. Charles put the entire town up for sale and sold it for a quarter of a million dollars; then he left town. Nellie was heart-broken, but never gave up hope that one day he would return and marry her. Charles died in 1955; Nellie died a couple years later of cancer. They both died childless and neither ever married. It's believed that Nellie haunts the inn, unable to accept the fact that her lover never returned.

The inn features 14 guest bedrooms. Be sure to request Nellie's room. The restaurant serves lunch and dinner with a variety of sandwiches, salads, and burgers. The Arrow Lounge offers a variety of cocktail drinks, draft and bottled beers, wines and soft drinks. On Halloween, they sponsor the "Monster Mash" costume party with food, drink, and prizes.

Paulding Light

Location: Paulding, Haight Township, Ontonagon County, Michigan
AKA: Dog Meadow Light, Watersmeet Light, Lights of Paulding, Paulding Ghost Light, Paulding Spook Light, or Paulding Mystery Light
GPS: 46°21'08"N 89°10'43.5"W

Directions:

- **From Watersmeet.** Drive 5.4 miles north on Hwy 45. Turn left on 5230 at Robbins Pond National Forest Campground sign. Drive .7 miles straight down the gravel road until it ends at a metal guardrail.

- **From Paulding.** Drive 4.2 miles south on Hwy 45. Take a sharp right on 5230 at Robbins Pond National Forest Campground sign. Drive .7 miles straight down the gravel road until it ends at a metal guardrail.

Ghost Lore

It's Michigan's most famous unsolved mystery, and it attracts curiosity seekers from around the world. On any given night, dozens of cars line the gravel road and wait patiently for the sun to set. At dusk a small dot of light appears on the distant horizon, and the onlookers gasp. The light grows in size and intensity and begins to dance and change color. It has an appearance reminiscent of someone carrying a lantern. The crowd watches in amazement as the light disappears and reappears throughout the night. A nearby National Forest sign tells the legend of the light:

> This is the location from which the famous Paulding Light can be observed. Legend explains its presence as a railroad brakeman's ghost, destined to remain forever at the sight of his untimely death. He continually waves his signal lantern as a warning to all who come to visit.

Visitors to the area frequently discover that the spook light is not the only mystery that lurks in the darkness.

- Strange noises and blood-curdling screams have been heard in the woods.

- Shadow people have been seen walking across the clearing.

- Apparitions of Native Americans have been reported.

- What appears to be the "Grim Reaper" has been seen floating across the road near the light.

- Photography has been known to capture anomalies of orbs, mists, and strange electrical entities.

- It's common for people to experience mechanical or electrical problems with their vehicles after visiting the observation area.

- Orbs and strange mists have been seen floating through the area.

- People have felt a sensation of energy or electricity.

- People have heard the sound of a phantom train passing by, although the railroad tracks were removed years ago.

- People have recorded EVPs in the area.

History

1966 –   The first documented sighting occurred when a group of teenagers reported the light to the local sheriff.

2004 –   Unexplained Research LLC investigated the light.

2010 –   Students from the Michigan Tech chapter of the Society of Photo-Optical Instrumentation Engineers (SPIE) investigated the light.

2010 –   The Syfy television series *Fact or Faked: Paranormal Files* conducted their own investigation.

Investigation

Our investigation discovered a great deal of misinformation surrounding this case. It's been said that the *Ripley's Believe It or Not!* television series investigated the light, and, after failing to explain it, offered $100,000 to anyone who could. There have been three incarnations of this program. The original series, on NBC, was initially hosted by Robert L. Ripley himself and ran from 1949 to 1950; the second series, on ABC, was hosted by Jack Palance, and ran from 1982-1986. A third series, on TBS, was hosted by Dean Cain and ran from 1999 to 2003. None of these programs investigated the Paulding Light, and the Ripley's franchise flatly denies it has ever offered a $100,000 reward.

It has also been claimed that the *Unsolved Mysteries* television series has investigated the light. This series has also had more than one incarnation. The first version was hosted by Robert Stack from 1987-2002; the second was hosted by Dennis Farina from 2008-2010. Neither series mentioned the Paulding Light. However, the first series did feature an investigation of Arkansas's Gurdon Light (see episode #317, air date December 16, 1994) which is similar to the Paulding Light, and people may have naturally confused the two.

Supposedly sightings of the light date back over a hundred years, to a time before the invention of the automobile, but the earliest *documented* sighting we could find only dates back to 1966. It was at this time that Highway 45 was rerouted to its current location, and the old road was abandoned and barricaded. At that time, the dead-end became a popular make-out spot, and that's when teenagers first began to report the light.

Author Chad Lewis viewing the light through a telescope

Paranormal Explanations

Over the years a number of explanations have been proposed for the Paulding Light. Some people believe the lights to be extraterrestrial UFOs; others view it as a religious manifestation of angels or something divine. But the most common explanations relate it to haunting activity. Numerous legends have arisen to explain the phenomenon. Many of these stories revolve around the railroad.

- **Brakeman.** According to the National Forest sign, the "official" story concerns a railroad brakeman (in other versions it was either a railroad watchman, signalman, switchman, or conductor). Supposedly a train was stalled on

the tracks after dark, and another train was rapidly approaching from behind. A heroic railroad worker stood on the tracks frantically waving his lantern in an attempt to stop the oncoming train when he was fatally crushed between the two trains (in other versions he was decapitated). There is disagreement amongst storytellers as to whether the accident occurred in the nineteenth or the twentieth century. Regardless, the Paulding Light is believed to be the ghost of the worker, still waving his lantern each night throughout eternity.

- **Engineer.** A railroad engineer was murdered nearby the tracks where the light is seen today. It's believed his spirit is manifested as a light.

- **Father.** A man with a lantern was frantically searching for his son who was lost in the woods after dark. The father was accidentally struck and killed by a train. His spirit still wanders the woods in search of his missing boy.

- **Children.** A boy and girl with flashlights were playing on the railroad tracks when they were killed by a train. They haunt the tracks while still carrying their flashlights.

- **Ghost Train.** A train derailed and crashed sometime in the late 1800s. There was at least one fatality. In some accounts, the light is a lantern carried by a ghostly conductor who watches over the crash site. In other versions, the light is the headlight of a phantom train.

- **Lumberjack.** A lumberjack was having an affair with a railroad engineer's wife. There was an angry confrontation between the two men which resulted in the engineer's murder. The light is said to be his wandering spirit, grieving that he lost his unfaithful wife to the lumberman.

- **Mail Carrier.** During the winter of 1870, a mail carrier was transporting mail through the swamp by dogsled. When he failed to arrive at his destination, a search party was dispatched. They found him and his dog team dead at the place where the Paulding Light is seen today. Supposedly he was ambushed and murdered by Indians. The light is believed to be his spirit searching for his dead dogs.

- **Native American.** The light is a ghostly manifestation of a dead Indian chief who is angry that the power lines run through his sacred land.

- **Miner.** The ghost of a copper miner—still wearing his miner's helmet with the attached carbide lamp—is believed to be the source of the Paulding Light.

Which, if any, of these stories is true? Most likely none of them. Thus far, we've been unable to verify the historicity of any of these events. After searching through archives of old newspapers, we couldn't find any news articles confirming the train wrecks, fatal accidents, or murders described in the above legends.

Scientific Explanations

Scientists have also been intrigued by the Paulding Light and have offered a number of scientific explanations for the phenomenon.

- **Radon Gas.** According to seismologists, thousands of years ago the Upper Peninsula was compressed under the weight of huge glaciers. After the ice retreated, the earth's crust expanded and cracked which may have caused radioactive incandescent gases to leak to the surface and emit a brilliant radioluminescence. *Problem: Tests conducted in the area with gas meters found normal levels of radiation.*

- **The Piezo-electric Effect.** Other seismologists have speculated that the Paulding Light is caused by the same mechanism that generates earthquake lights. The piezo-electric effect results from tectonic stress. When quartz is under pressure it can generates a luminescent electric charge. *Problem: The Upper Peninsula is a very low seismic activity area. Also, EMF meters detect no unusual electromagnetic spikes in the region.*

- **Swamp Gas.** Some scientists dismiss the light as being a will-o'-the-wisp. They argue that methane is produced by the decomposition of organic matter in swamps, bogs, and marshes, and oxidation of the methane might cause it to become luminescent. *Problem: In the winter the ground is frozen and covered with snow, which would prevent the decomposition of organic matter. The Paulding Light is seen year round, even in the dead of winter. In addition, tests have been conducted in the summer using gas detectors, and levels were found to be low.*

- **Lighthouse.** It has been suggested that the light is the beacon from a distant lighthouse on the coast of Lake Superior. *Problem: If it is, it would have to be a phantom lighthouse. The only lighthouse in that direction is Fourteen Mile Point Lighthouse, located almost 50 miles away; however, it was deactivated and abandoned in 1934 and destroyed by fire in 1984. Another problem with this explanation is that the Paulding Light does not have the regularity of a lighthouse beacon.*

- **Headlights.** The most popular explanation is that the light is actually the headlights and taillights of vehicles five miles away on Highway 45. In 2010, students from the Michigan Tech chapter of the Society of Photo-Optical Instrumentation

Engineers (SPIE) used a telescope to examine the light. What they observed were the distant headlights of a car on the highway. They declared the mystery to be officially solved. *Problem: Six years earlier, Unexplained Research LLC had already conducted its own investigation of the Paulding Light. As members of the research team, we had also examined the light through a telescope and were able to identify headlights and taillights of vehicles on the highway north of Paulding. However, those more familiar with the light informed us that what we were gazing upon wasn't the Paulding Light. According to them, the authentic Paulding Light had not been seen in several years. What they described seeing in the past was a light so brilliant that they were unable to look directly at it. It would sometimes travel the full length of the valley, weaving its way around the power line poles. On occasion it would actually enter the observation area and "light up the forest like a stadium," as one eyewitness put it. In 2010, the Syfy channel's* Fact or Faked: Paranormal Files *series also visited Paulding and conducted an investigation with their sophisticated equipment (see Season 1, Episode 105, "Blazing Horizon/Rollover"). They had police officers shut down*

traffic on Highway 45 in both directions. To their amazement, in the absence of any headlights, the ghost light still made an appearance. At the conclusion of their investigation they declared the phenomenon to be "unexplainable."

Although there are numerous theories, no one has yet unraveled the mystery. That's what makes it worth the drive to see the light firsthand.

On a side note, after our initial visit to the Paulding Light, we were driving back home late at night when the dashboard lights on our vehicle failed. A short time later, we were pulled over by the police because our taillights and brake lights were also not functioning. After shutting off the car and restarting it, everything worked fine. We had never had this problem with the car in the past and never had it again since. Later we recalled the warning people had given us about vehicles commonly experiencing mechanical and electrical malfunctions after having visited the Paulding Light.

Tip. If you arrive after dark, be sure to dim your headlights after you turn off of Highway 45. Your brights can be annoying to the people who are already there.

The Dare. If you walk toward the Paulding Light, it will vanish from your sight, yet mysteriously remain visible to those remain at the observation area.

About the Authors

Chad Lewis is a paranormal investigator for Unexplained Research LLC, with a Master's Degree in Applied Psychology from the University of Wisconsin-Stout. Chad has spent years traveling the globe researching ghosts, strange creatures, crop formations, and UFOs. Chad is a former state director for the Mutual UFO Network and has worked with BLT Research on crop circle investigations. Chad is the organizer of the *Unexplained* Conferences and hosted *The Unexplained* paranormal radio talk show and television series.

Terry Fisk is also a paranormal investigator for Unexplained Research LLC and lecturer on death and the afterlife. He is a shamanic Buddhist practitioner and member of the Foundation for Shamanic Studies who studied Philosophy and Religion at the University of Wisconsin. Terry co-hosted *The Unexplained* paranormal radio talk show and directed *The Unexplained* television series. He has investigated hauntings with famed medium Allison DuBois and TV psychic Chip Coffey.

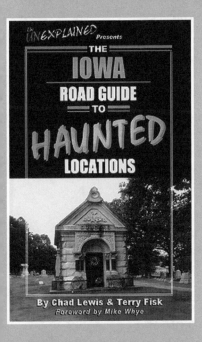
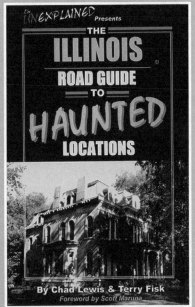

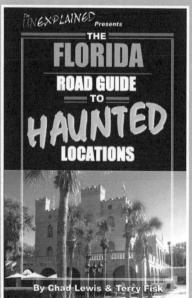

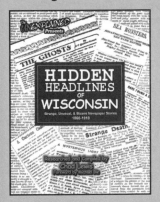
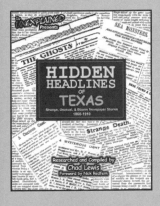
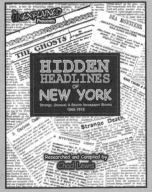

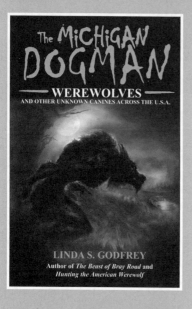

The UNEXPLAINED *the* **Presents**

"The Unexplained" Sweatshirt

COLOR: Black

SIZES: M, L, XL, 2XL

Hooded. 100% cotton. "The Unexplained with Chad Lewis and Terry Fisk" on front.

"The Unexplained" Tee shirt

COLOR: Black

SIZES: M, L, XL, 2XL

Short-sleeved. 100% cotton. "The Unexplained with Chad Lewis and Terry Fisk" on front.

www.unexplainedresearch.com

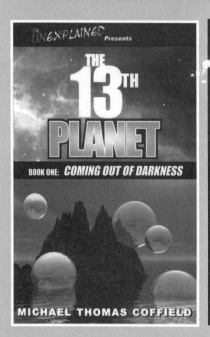